Speaking,
Listening,
Understanding

SPIRITUALITY AND SOCIAL RENEWAL

. . . .

Vision in Action

The Veiled Pulse of Time

Speaking, Listening, Understanding

The Art of Creating Conscious Conversation

Heinz Zimmermann

Translated by James H. Hindes

Lindisfarne Books

This edition was translated by James H. Hindes from German
Sprechen, Zuhören, Verstehen in Erkenntnis- und Entscheidungsprozessen,
Verlag Freies Geistesleben, Stuttgart, Germany, 1991.

© Association of Waldorf Schools of North America, 1996, 2004

Published by Lindisfarne Books
400 Main Street, Great Barrington, MA 01230
www.lindisfarne.org

Library of Congress Cataloging-in-Publication Data

Zimmermann, Heinz, 1937–
 [Sprechen, Zuhören, Verstehen in Erkenntnis- und
Entscheidungsprozessen. English]
 Speaking, listening, understanding : the art of creating
conscious conversation / Heinz Zimmermann ; translated by
James H. Hindes.
    p. cm. – (Spirituality and social renewal)
 Includes bibliographical references.
 ISBN 0-940262-75-4
 1. Conversation analysis. 2. Communication in small groups.
I.Title. II. Series.
P95.45.Z5613   1996
302.3'46—dc20   96-14805
                                                          CIP

Contents

Preface

The book you hold in your hands is the result of lectures, workshops, and courses given in many places. Rather than the dynamics of group psychology, my starting point for these has always been the artistic aspects of language. I attempted to become conscious of the various aspects of the phenomena of language with the help of methodical description. Consciousness of these phenomena provides the basis for training in conversation.

This book results from many years' experience in a "self-administered" Waldorf School. During those years, I watched the decision-making process unfold through innumerable conversations and committee meetings. It is my hope that this short text can serve as an aid for those seeking to increase their conversational ability. Only such increased competence will enable us to raise the human interaction taking place in any conversation to a higher level.

Heinz Zimmermann

MARCH 1991

Introduction

When we think back on what we have experienced in past conversations, memories arise in us that are unique and commonplace, blessed and horrid. All of us can think of conversations that enriched us with a profound human encounter, or interviews and examinations that still pain us. We can remember a community effort or group struggle to understand some problem, and the feeling of being completely understood when a solution suddenly blossomed. Then, too, we can remember times when we struggled unsuccessfully for hours, or tried all evening to get in a word. Such memories clearly show that conversations have a decisive impact on our lives. They accompany us daily and reflect our relationships with other people. To measure the full social significance of conversation, we need only stop and think of how many conversational contacts we had during the day just passed. Improving our ability to converse means improving our ability to interact socially. We can give our partners-in-conversation opportunities to develop themselves, arrive at insights, find solutions, and feel supported; or, we can use conversation solely to develop and validate ourselves. We can use words to argue with or to skewer someone—to defend, counter, manipulate, defeat, or kill—or we can use words to lift up, support, protect, unite, bless, and heal. In conversation, we can exercise power or send forth love. But, in our ordinary lives this is not a conscious process; it usually happens instinctively.

Since ancient times, guidance or schooling in linguistic competence has existed, using speech exercises, training in the development of style, schooling in dialectics, and so forth. Most instructions of this kind, however, are primarily concerned with the speaker and are one-sided in their purpose, asking only "How can I argue so that my words are convincing?" Thus, the question of power generally stands in the foreground: "How can I assert myself, how can I convince others, how can I win a discussion?" These aspects do, of course, belong to any training in speaking. But in social life, and therefore also in conversation, we are never only concerned with one isolated individual or another, but rather with reciprocal relations. Any training must take this fact into account. Many of the steps involved in conversation training must be taken by individuals alone. Yet, the path of training can begin in the community where it is to be practiced only when individuals join together in conversation. This form of schooling in conversation rarely occurs. However, as we will see later, it can lead to significant results. In this book I am primarily interested in those group conversations seeking insight and knowledge that can lead to decisions. I shall be dealing with groups, whose members are essentially equals—there are many outstanding books available that deal with therapeutic conversation. To begin with we must make the elements of conversation explicit, from various points of view. How does a conversation arise? What are its foundations? What are the forms and stages of conversation? In dealing with these questions, we will discover starting places for our training quite naturally.

Later, we will summarize and explore the area of training itself.

CHAPTER 1

The Elements of Conversation

A common example shows us the basic elements involved at the beginning of a conversation:

A: "Now, where have you put the newspaper?"
B: "It's lying on the table."
A: "Thank you. I see it now."

"A" first wants to know something and therefore asks
a question. "B" answers the question, satisfies his or her
partner, who then formulates a grateful confirmation. It
is clear that the activity of speaking, listening, and understanding constantly alternate between partners. The
common element is the language that is spoken, heard,
and understood. The process involved in conversation is
often compared with the "obvious" technical "sender-re-
ceiver" model. The speaker sends the message in a common code—the forms of the language—and the re-
ceiver deciphers the code, that is, understands what the
sender wants to convey. This model, however, does not
take into account the relationship that lives between the
partners and continuously influences the conversation.
· In reality, it is by no means the case that the speaker is
on one side and the listener on the other; actually, "listening" affects the speaker as much as it does the listener

and, conversely, "speaking" affects the listener as much as the speaker. Who of us has not had the experience of wanting to say something but then changing our intended words (or even foregoing them) because of the wordless behavior of the other person? Or perhaps we were actually able to say things of which we had never even thought before.

The ways in which partners in conversation affect one another depend in large measure on how they relate to one another. Imagine that, in our example, a married couple is speaking. Perhaps they have grown accustomed to one another and now sometimes experience friction in such everyday events as, for example, when the newspaper is not in its usual place. Spoken in the appropriate tone of voice, the word "now" in the sentence "Now, where have you put the newspaper?" enables the man to express his irritation. We could easily imagine that the woman is not reacting to the objective information but rather to the irritation we have described. Then this minor exchange could lead to fullblown marital strife. We see from this that we must consider the context of contributions to a conversation in a rich context of relationships— for example, in the partners' relationship to one another or in their relationship to the situation.

Perhaps the husband in our example is looking for his newspaper after breakfast. The location is determined. It is the married couple's apartment, at the breakfast table. The time, too, is determined: it is early morning. We know, too, the conversation's specific circumstances and goal: the solution to an everyday problem. These circumstances provide the "soil," so to speak, out of which the conversation will grow. Let us therefore turn our attention to this field.

Conversation takes place at a specific location, within a specific time frame, and influenced by other "givens" such as weather, clothing, and so on. The actual cause or purpose of a conversation may be considered a fourth precondition. All of these, together with the participants and their mutual relationships, create the body into which the conversation can descend. Just as the physical body provides an opportunity for the soul and spirit to manifest, so too do the preconditions, the "givens," of any conversation provide the opportunity for a conversation to manifest. The more a body can absorb and express the soul and spirit of a human being, the more perfectly it serves as his or her instrument. The same is true of conversation. In everyday conversations, the given conditions function more or less naturally. But, as soon as we go beyond this everyday stage—for example, to seek knowledge in a community setting, or try to make decisions communally, or simply want to encounter another human being at a higher level—then our success largely depends on how consciously we work with the preconditions (the "givens") in order to make them fruitful for the conversation. We will now describe these individual factors in greater detail, trying to make visible certain starting points for the kind of training in conversation that will increase our ability to converse competently.

The Location

Let us first imagine ourselves in various extreme situations. This will help us to appreciate fully how strongly the location of a conversation works to determine its style. The location of a conversation can help or hinder conversation; it can make certain forms of conversation possible, or impossible. We speak differently when we are traveling at one hundred miles an hour in the large viewing car of a train than we do in a room high up in a tower; we speak differently in a tent than in a cellar. We breathe and speak differently in a cramped room than in a light-filled expanse. Walls and ceiling enclose and protect us from distraction. We can even become sensitive to the effects of windows being open rather than closed during a conversation. In short, the arrangement of the room in which we are speaking can affect us. Furthermore, some things can be discussed better during a walk than sitting in a quiet room. Geographical location is also important. Since ancient times, certain locations have been felt to be particularly suitable for spiritual life and, for this reason, as old legends witness, cultic centers were built on such locations. Mountains, plains, ocean landscapes, the nearness of nature and urban centers, whether we are in the north or the south—all deeply influence the sheath within which a conversation takes place.

The seating in the room is also essential. It makes a large difference whether or not the participants all see one another face to face. Do they sit, stand, or are they reclining? Are they comfortable or uncomfortably crowded? Are they hunched over wooden stools or sunk into upholstery so deep that they can extricate themselves only with great effort? The influence that participants can exert on the direction of conversation is also somewhat limited by their location in the room relative to the group leader. In conversations intended to reach decisions, we can see that the seats directly across from the conversational leader, as well as those immediately next to him or her, have greater influence than others. We can also observe how certain people instinctively seek out such seats and do not allow themselves to be driven out of them easily. We also know the custom whereby the head of the family occupies the place at the narrow end of the table, facing the door, so that he rules the room. Furthermore, we know that in earlier times teachers stood on a podium so they could survey the entire class, and judges are still seated above both the accused and the witnesses. Conversations with such preconditions are already fixed in a one-sided way by the given division of roles.

Time

Time has just as great an influence on a conversation as its location. Conversations held in the morning have an entirely different character than those held in the evening or at night. We speak differently depending upon whether it is winter or summer. It makes a difference if we decide something at 11:00 P.M. after a long discussion without a break or if we make the decision at 5:00 P.M. when we are still fresh. How long we can continue a conversation without a break depends on the people and, above all, on the conversation's theme and intended goal. Usually, in guided conversations, we do not pay enough attention to the need for pauses at appropriate intervals. In the case of particularly important decisions, the personal contacts made during breaks can allow misunderstandings and frictions to be cleared away in the more relaxed atmosphere of the break. As a result, after such a break, participants can concentrate entirely on the objective problem at hand. Frequent short breaks make for healthy conversation. The more tired the participants, the less they can concentrate and the more the course of the conversation is influenced by bodily emotions and disturbances. When it comes to forming a successful conversation, breaks and pauses can be of decisive importance.

Other Considerations

Aside from considerations of place and time, other factors can influence conversation: for example, the weather, the atmosphere, the temperature, and so on. People converse differently in bathing suits than in smoking jackets. The course of a conversation that is planned and anticipated will follow a different path than one that is unplanned—for instance, one conducted standing in line at a supermarket or in an elevator. Many other similar accompanying circumstances could also be imagined.

Occasion and Purpose

The circumstances of a conversation are often related to the cause that initially occasioned the conversation. Consideration of this cause brings us closer to the heart of our question. If, when riding in a train, we ask those traveling in the same carriage with us where they are coming from, we are not asking an indiscreet question. Rather, we are simply seeking to make contact with others so as to shorten our traveling time. Speaking of the weather or discussing the region we are traveling through is only meant to lead us into conversation. The situation is quite different in the case of scientific conversations to which we come prepared to seek insight, understanding, and knowledge. These are conversations that are clearly framed from the outset. Because such conversations are meant to achieve a set goal, we have chairpeople, agendas, and individuals designated as leaders who will guide the proceedings.

A good example of such a consciously planned conversation would be a corporate meeting at which production goals are to be established for the following year. In the case of courtroom examinations and interrogations not only is the framework limiting the conversation already set, but the distribution of roles is also settled. The opposite of this is a personal conversation between friends who meet voluntarily to simply talk to one another. Conversations at official receptions or semi-official cocktail parties, where everyone is holding a glass of champagne, munching on salty crackers and simultaneously conversing with others, requires a gift of gallant superficiality in social interactions. Here too, of course, conventions can break down and interesting conversations can arise. Everything depends upon a proper estimation of the possibilities provided by the setting. It makes no sense to carry the mood of a spur-of-the-moment conversation into a serious conversation that is part of an institutional decision-making process. It is equally senseless, however, to admonish a family member—or a person one has just met and is getting to know—that he or she should stay with the theme.

The Participants and their Mutual Relationships

Participants in a family discussion or in a conversation among friends have a mutual familiarity with one another before the conversation starts. They know all their fellow participants' unique characteristics. When opening a new topic of discussion, a person in such a conversation knows from the outset how the various members will react. The situation is similar in discussion groups that are created by a work context where many decisions must be made in community and the partners know one another well. Here there are exchanges in the discussion process that seem to unfold with almost ritual predictability. One knows that when A says something B will react in a certain way. C will then speak up and support B. D will then attempt to help A, and so on.

Structures such as these can, of course, be eliminated, but only after they have become conscious. Conversations between people who have just met and are getting to know one another through the medium of conversation look very different from those in which everyone knows each other well. Sometimes, depending upon the purpose of a conversation, one can hear contributions that have no other purpose than to present the speaker to the others in the best possible light. For example, if I notice that everyone except me has already spoken, I will perhaps bring up something that I might otherwise never have mentioned simply to make myself noticeable, paying the expected enrollment fee, so to speak. Perhaps I am careful in my statements, cramped even, because I am not yet able to estimate the other participants' reactions. Here we see a factor that has a dampening effect on conversation, one that disappears as soon as people know and recognize one another better. But, if this is the case, then we are once again threatened by the danger mentioned above—that the contributions to the conversation become predictable, even in their sequence. If the participants know each other too well or do not know each other well enough, it is difficult for conversations to unfold freely in a creative manner.

The number of the participants greatly affects the character of a conversation. While a conversation between two people can have a particularly intimate character, the character of the conversation in a larger group depends to a great extent on whether everyone is able to express themselves freely, and whether everyone can see each other. The individual people involved and the theme chosen will also determine what kind of leadership is required to guide the conversation. Some people are inhibited from speaking in front of others if only ten people are present. The larger the number, the more organization and form are required. Also, beginning with a certain number (as a rule, about twenty), the hidden principle of representation takes over in groups. This means that some participants speak on behalf of others.

In order to create a productive, homogeneous environment among participants, we must be aware of the forces that threaten homogeneity. These forces are primarily the various relationships between the individuals and subgroups within the group. Age, sex, interpersonal relations, profession, nationality, language, interests, temperament, character, and a common destiny are community-building elements that can create smaller groups that then threaten to divide people in the larger group.

Because it plays an important role in work settings, there is one relationship in particular I would like to mention here: the community created out of common memories. Common childhood experiences can establish very strong relationships. When people have gone to school together they speak differently to one another than when they have just met. Common experiences formed by common deeds create a powerful bond between people. Every time a school, a company, or any organization requiring group effort is founded, the individuals involved share common experiences. Such common memories, when shared later, can lead to serious difficulties if they are not understood. Those who join the venture later often feel themselves unequal partners in conversation with the pioneers. For their part, the founders fear that their earlier accomplishments are not sufficiently recognized and valued. Therefore they attempt to institutionalize the community of founders. The situation can become catastrophic if decisions are made at meetings in which the participants are ostensibly equal but where, in reality, nothing happens without the blessing of the pioneers.

Now that we have considered some of the facts and preconditions that determine the quality of conversation from the outside, we can turn to the central questions of how do contributions to conversation arise, and how are they received by others?

Conversational Exercises

The following exercises (and those following subsequent chapters) were developed by Jon McAlice in collaboration with Heinz Zimmermann in a circle of friends who met regularly to work toward a deeper understanding of conversation as a social art. The exercises were developed through looking back on conversations focused on various themes. They serve both to heighten individual awareness of the spatio-temporal flow of conversation, as well as to awaken abilities needed for actively co-creative conversation.

All of these exercises have been worked with over time and they have proven viable—none are abstract

constructions. They focus on the concrete development of abilities that play deciding roles in whether or
not a conversation becomes a truly human meeting
place, and those of us who have worked with these exercises regularly, have witnessed their contribution. Of
course, no single exercise or group of exercises can
work miracles. Individuals must grow consciously toward grasping and working formatively with such a process, which takes time. This is especially true within the
sphere of human interaction.

The source of all individual development lies in the
will. No exercise can bear fruit unless it is worked with
repetitively. An exercise begins to stimulate the trans-
formational process only when we become actively involved in it—we must "get our feet wet." There is an an-
ecdote I once heard concerning René Querido, a
Waldorf teacher. During one of his teacher training
courses, he opened the morning's work by saying, "Today I want to tell you which meditation is the most important meditation for your work." After a moment's
pause, the atmosphere ripe with attentive expectation,
he continued, "The most important meditation for
your work is the meditation that you *do!*"

Most of us have, at some point or other, had a chance
to discover obstacles lying in the path of self-education.
Generally, we see that it is relatively difficult to continue,
and we either forget that we actually decided to do a certain exercise for a given period of time, or we discover
that we have developed a certain antipathy for the exercise. It is easy to imagine that these obstacles along our
path of inner development also arise when we begin to
practice with other people. If we remember how much
effort it took to overcome these hindrances, we then
have a sense of what is required when a circle of people

decide to practice together. One possibility for overcoming any arising inertia is to approach the exercises in much the same way as a connoisseur approaches a fine meal, or as a music lover listens to a good symphony.

The following exercises have been worked with in different rhythms—weekly, monthly, and so on. A bimonthly rhythm of intensive five- to six-hour meetings has proven to be quite productive, as long as work is done by individuals between meetings. Of course, each group will need to find its own rhythm.

Before turning to the exercises themselves, there is one aspect that we should bear in mind. In his *Letters Concerning the Aesthetic Education of the Human Being,* Schiller spoke of the nature and importance of artistic play. He said that "a human being is only fully human when at play." An understanding of the role of "aesthetic play" in the human being's inner development has largely been lost. Schiller found the source of a human being's ongoing cultivation of spiritual potentials in the joy of artistic exercise. Play is the activity through which we create an intentional and dynamic balance between the poles of natural necessity and stringent idealism. When we approach play in this sense, we see its complete dependence on individual activity. The satisfaction it brings is not the satisfaction of passive consumption, but of artistic effort.

The suggested exercises speak to the artist living in each of us. Once we awaken this artist, we will discover manifold variations and imagine new exercises we can try out and work with.

Rhythm and Movement: Clapping and Stamping

- Try to achieve an even-paced, uniform clapping while moving in a circle.

- Focus attention on the clapping itself, then on the movement perceptible between claps.

- Differentiate between the quality experienced when clapping close to one's body and the quality when attempting to "hear" the motion of the clap as something moving past at arm's length.

There are many ways of modulating this uniform clapping:

- Loud, soft. With fluid transitions to crescendo 'and back to pianissimo, with abrupt changes. We can let the clapping grow so soft that it disappears, still following the motion of the clapping, and picking it up at will.

- Fast, slow. With fluid transitions between clapping faster until it races around the circle like a ball of fire, and then bringing it again to rest.

- We can also give spatial wave-forms to the motion. These can travel around the circle or back and forth across the circle.

- A new vista of possible exercises is opened when we begin to consciously vary the clapping rhythms.

- We can have a basic rhythm which goes around the circle—short, short, long; short, short, long; and so on.

- We can agree on a basic beat, and then each can improvise a given number of measures.

- A variation of this exercise could be that the next participant first repeats what his or her predecessor clapped before continuing.

- Another is to listen for the various contributions as a "melody"—to pick up inwardly what has been clapped, and develop it further.

- One member of the circle can clap a measure, and then the rest of the circle could try to repeat it. There are no previous agreements as to who claps next, and we simply try to keep the process—the "melody"—going, in dialogue between "presenter" and "choir."

- The circle can be dissolved, and individuals move freely, aimlessly throughout the room. Whoever takes on the role of precentor moves when clapping, and the choir stands still. When clapping, the choir moves, and the precentor stands still.

Most of these exercises can also be done with stamping instead of clapping. One exercise, however, is especially for the feet:

- In a circle again, the first person stamps with the right foot. The person standing to the left stamps with the right foot. The first stamps with the left foot; the second stamps with the left foot. The same sequence is then repeated by the second and third persons, and so on.

All of the exercises can be done "blind"—either with closed eyes, or by those in the circle facing outward.

CHAPTER 2

The Miracle of Speaking

How does a contribution to a conversation arise?

The most varied stimuli can move us to speak. We may encounter someone and greet them; or perhaps we want to know something and pose a question; or perhaps we experience something powerfully and then express our feelings about it. We might formulate a thought to explain to someone what is going on around us. A conversation always arises when what has already been said stimulates me to make a contribution of my own.

Often, I myself am unaware of what moved me to speak. The form in which what I said existed in my consciousness before being expressed is equally vague. It seems to exist either as an indefinite feeling, or a will impulse, or a complex of mental pictures and ideas, or, in rare instances, as a thought content or idea. The great question is how this soul content is transformed into understandable forms of speech. Usually, unless we have observed ourselves "from outside," so to speak, there is little we can say about this. However, if we simply consider the sentence "I want to say something" more closely, we can clarify the question.

We begin with the intention of the words, "I want." This is followed by a content, a "something" that is to be revealed through the medium of language. I, intention, and content then melt together into a linguistic expression— "I want" - "to say" - "something."

How does something that lives within us become something sense perceptible outside of us? Through self-observation, we find that the process contains many different elements. These we can illustrate through the following examples.

Two Examples

Think of a young man who wants to declare his love to his beloved. In the quiet of his room he considers how to begin the conversation, trying out various formulations of the decisive sentences. Much is discarded, many turns of phrase are preferred, some are dropped again. The young man imagines many possible reactions, considering what he might then say in response. Then he actually meets the girl and from the beginning everything is quite different than he had imagined. A mere trifle can overthrow his whole plan and the rest is stammering.

What is happening here? The conscious will to formulate apparently capitulates before the emotional excitement that hinders or blocks the flow of speech. We can see from this that speaking is an event occurring in time and is formed by the tension between consciousness and unconscious impulses. Consciousness is connected to our waking life of thoughts. Here we strive for a calm overview and clarity. The flow of language, however, is also connected to the half-conscious or unconscious kinetic forces in us, which strive for the dissolution of solid forms, which seek life, creativity, and movement.

Imagine that you had to give a verbal presentation to a large group of people—a lecture perhaps or a keynote address to open a celebration. You could, of course, write down everything you wanted to say and then simply read it aloud or memorize and then recite it. In this case, the speech would carry the indelible imprint of the past. The speech act taking place in the present would be limited to the vocalization of words formulated in the past. Listeners perceive this immediately. They notice when a speaker is not living completely in his or her formulation.

Public speakers occasionally depart from their prepared texts and speak spontaneously whenever supplemental material occurs to them. When this happens, we can see how listeners immediately become more attentive because they sense that something is being said that is alive in the moment of speaking. Even if the content is not new, the new formulation, freshly created in the moment, will be filled with life. In ancient times, speakers prepared their formulations down to the last detail and then learned them by heart, rehearsing their gestures, mimicry, and tone of voice so that their speeches could be compared to dramatic presentations.

Let us assume that we prepare the content of a speech thoroughly but then base our actual formulation on only a few key words outlined on paper; or even seek what we shall say entirely out of the moment. We then experience at an existential level the battle described above between thoughts and ideas on the one hand and the flow of language, feelings, and impulses on the other. At the same time, there is always the fear that we would no longer know what to say next or that grammar or the choice of words might suddenly abandon us. Here we experience the limits of our consciousness as a dead end. Only if we entrust ourselves to our own stream of speech can we pass through this block. Then we can experience how speaking leads us to thoughts that may never have occurred to us before. Then, too, we are in a position to react to our listeners and are also helped by them.

Speaking Produces Thought

In his essay "On the Gradual Preparation of Thoughts While Speaking," Heinrich von Kleist brilliantly describes the interaction between form and movement:

> If you want to know something and cannot find it through meditation, my dear, clever friend, then I recommend you discuss it with the very next acquaintance you happen to meet. He or she need not be especially brilliant; nor do I mean that you should ask your acquaintance about it. On the contrary, you yourself should tell your friend about it first. I can see from the wide eyes now answering me that you were taught when young to speak only of things you already understand. But at that age, however, you were probably speaking impertinently and wanted to teach others. Now I want you to speak with the prudent intention of teaching yourself. Thus, in different cases, different rules of behavior can perhaps coexist quite well. The French say "l'appétit vient en mangeant" (appetite comes as you eat), a saying that is based on experience. This is a true saying, one that remains true even when parodied as "l'idée vient en parlant" (the idea comes as you speak).
>
> I often sit at my desk over a stack of documents and seek the best approach to judge a complicated legal conflict. In my efforts to understand a matter

in which my deepest being is involved, I usually look into my lamp as if toward the brightest point. Or, if an algebra problem comes my way, I seek the first step, the equation that expresses the given relationships and then leads to the solution after a few simple calculations. But, lo and behold, if I speak to my sister who is sitting and working behind me, then I discover what I would perhaps never have found, even after hours of brooding. It is not as if she actually told me, for she knows neither the law nor has studied Euler or Kaestner. [1]

Nor did she lead me with a series of clever questions to the decisive point, although this may occasionally be the case. The fact is I have some kind of a dim notion that is distantly related in some way to what I seek. And if I can just make an audacious enough start then, even as I speak, pressured by the need to find an ending, my mind will transform my confused notion into full clarity to such an extent that the knowledge I seek, to my surprise, is ready by the time the period comes at the end of the sentence. I mix in inarticulate sounds, draw out the connecting words, speak in appositions where none are necessary and generally employ any trick that will gain me the time I need to construct my idea in the workshop of reason. [2]

---

1. Leonhard Euler and Abraham Kästner were well-known eighteenth century mathematicians.
2. Heinrich von Kleist, *An Abyss Deep Enough: Letters of Heinrich von Kleist*, ed./trans., Phillip B. Miller (NY: E.P. Dutton, 1982). (Present extract was translated by J. Hindes.)

Speaking becomes a means of outlining an indeterminate idea—a technique for reaching out and taking hold of it. How difficult this can be at times may be observed when we are struggling to understand something. We may work on a difficult problem for a long time before a solution suddenly occurs to us. It "falls" into our consciousness from "above," entirely filling us. But then we must immediately unfold it in time, or it will inadvertently escape from us again. Often it is when we first try to explain what we have grasped to another person that we notice that the words are lacking or, at the least, that we require many words to make ourselves understood. But conversation, soliloquy (inner dialogue), or a diary entry can calm emotions and organize intense memories and impressions. We seek to understand and master that part of world events that has taken hold of us. Many conversations give relief to participants because they are able to "talk themselves out." In this sense, speaking itself has a harmonizing effect.

Observation shows us that our relationship to speech can vary enormously according to the degree to which we identify with what is being said. Events that directly take hold of us—an invitation, a joyous surprise—are expressed in forms of speech that express our spontaneous reaction to what has been said. An exclamation, for example, will sound very different from driving instructions given in a more distant tone of voice. Appropriately enough, we unite with our momentary feelings and will impulses more strongly than with our thoughts and images. Our tone of voice, more than anything else, reveals our inner relationship to what we are saying.

Meeting the Spirit of Language

Let us consider from yet another angle the process whereby we translate our inner life—thoughts, images, feelings and emotions—into linguistic form. The quotation from Kleist already shows us that we never proceed additively. We do not reflect upon the sequence of words, and even less on the grammatical form. Rather, we set out from a wholeness that is first felt unconsciously and then differentiated into individual sentences, words, and forms. This process of transformation takes place more or less automatically. It is an expression of the fact that, in the beginning, we also absorbed language into ourselves unconsciously, through imitation and differentiation.

No adult taught us all the logical relationships that live in syntax and are expressed in language. Having heard them spoken by others, we unconsciously united ourselves with these relationships by actively speaking them within ourselves. They live on in us as abilities. But these stop when we reflect on them. This leads us to acknowledge that something living and important works in us through our mother tongue. We make use of it without at first even understanding it. Accordingly, we may understand the previously mentioned example of a free or blocked flow of language as a question of being more or less devoted to this living stream of language, and of entrusting ourselves to it to a greater or lesser extent. We can observe in ourselves how, when we are formulating our words spontaneously, our consciousness swings back and forth between the content we wish to utter and its linguistic form. While perceiving our own formulations, we constantly correct, expand, and modify them. The process of speaking would be extremely difficult if we were unable to hear ourselves as we spoke.

Here we arrive at a miracle, one that confirms our inclination to speak of a real spirit of language at work within us. Until now, we have considered the linguistic process as if it were exclusively an activity in our consciousness. There is, however, also a physiological side to the process that largely escapes our waking consciousness of normal speech: For every word we wish to speak, our speech organism must be enervated in such a way that an entire prearranged sequence of sounds becomes audible.

For example, consider the word *same*. The *s* sound is created by placing the tongue lightly against the teeth and exhaling; the *a* by holding the mouth partly opened with the tongue beginning more or less in the middle of the mouth and moving forward but not resting on the roof of the mouth directly behind the top teeth; the *m* is created with the lips closed, the air escaping from the lungs through the nose, thereby causing the nasal passages to vibrate. Although this linguistic description is far from complete, it is nevertheless quite clear that we would never get beyond a stammer if we had to form all of the sounds required by language consciously. And we have not even considered the more detailed and delicate bodily processes. In his work, *The Biological Foundations of Language*, Eric Lenneberg writes:

> If we bear in mind that the muscles of the thorax, of the abdominal walls, of the neck and face, of the larynx, pharynx, and mouth are usually all coordinated, then it becomes clear that over one hundred muscles must be controlled from a central location. Since the transition from one sound to another ultimately depends upon muscle control actions, a

command must be given to every muscle fourteen times per second: to contract, relax, or maintain tension. [3]

Lenneberg then illustrates the connection between the production of individual vocal sounds and the activity of certain muscles through time. From this, it becomes evident "that the new positions assumed by the muscles are not entered upon simultaneously, but rather that different groups of muscles are subject to special temporal control." He concludes that several hundred individual muscle events occur every second. "It is clear [he writes] that the activation of so many muscles in so short a period of time could not depend upon will alone. There must be some kind of automatic mechanism—entire chains of events that are pre-programmed and take place automatically."

We prefer to see in this phenomenon, not automatic mechanisms, but rather the work and organization of a living spirit of language, with whom we can create a more or less conscious relationship through training and development. In either case, the processes involved in speaking are closely connected to those involved in movement, from mimicry and gesture to breathing and the delicate muscle activity involved in the speech act itself.

As speaking human beings, we place ourselves between movement and thought. While our consciousness is clear in thinking, motor activity occurs unconsciously. Speech is an activity that oscillates back and forth, mediating between unconscious motor activity and the process of conscious thought formation. The actual

---

3. Eric Lenneberg, *The Biological Foundations of Language* (NY: Wiley, 1967).

medium of speech is our flow of breath, which is subject to a rhythm that reflects, in a subtle way, the two opposite poles of consciousness just mentioned. In-breathing is a delicate waking; it conveys consciousness of thought. Out-breathing is a delicate falling asleep, a surrendering of oneself to one's surroundings. We form our speech with the stream of air we are exhaling and thereby accompany our speaking with an unconscious element.

As we make the transition from speaker to listener in what follows, we shall find this relationship to breathing illuminated from another angle.

Conversational Exercises

Greek Wrestling

In his course on drama, Rudolf Steiner spoke about the relation between the five classical Greek sports and the development of expressive ability.[4] Wrestling is the third of these sports. We have found that the wrestling exercises developed from Steiner's indications help to heighten awareness of different movement qualities, which can then be discovered again on a higher level in conversational interaction.[5]

---

4. Rudolf Steiner, *Speech and Drama* (Hudson, NY: Anthroposophic Press, 1959), lecture given September 5, 1924.
5. Such exercises, developed by Count Bothmer, are known as "Bothmer Gymnastics" in Europe and as "Spacial Dynamics" in North America.

Greek wrestling can help to enliven the activity that "goes on 'below' the head—the 'wit' of the body, or rather the wit that moves the body." In wrestling we learn "to 'read' the activity of the other's will," as we feel each other push or pull.[6]

[Publisher's addendum:

• Place your hands against those of an "adversary" and, holding the tension, test each other's forces; turn with each other in a simple wrestling. Let there be a harmonious flow to it to begin with, and then gradually exaggerate the extremes of form and energy, fire and water, etc., in a dramatic interchange. Listen to each other with your hands (it can also be done with two wooden rods extending between you). This should not be seen as just symbolic. Observe each other; work with the quality of the conversation. Without a question between you—a basic "Who are you?"—the movement will be completely empty. It needs to be continually recreated out of the space between you.[7]

• A mime developed from wrestling: Two characters are on either side of a river. The sound of

---

6. Peter Bridgmont, *Liberation of the Actor* (London: Temple Lodge, 1992), pp. 29, 30.
7. Paul Matthews, *Sing Me the Creation: A Sourcebook for Poets and Teachers and for All Who Wish to Develop the Life of Imagination* (Stroud, UK: Hawthorn Press, 1994), p. 72.

the water drowns their voices, but the gesture of one seeks to encourage the other to cross the river on the stepping stones, while the other indicates reluctance to do so. Their conversation is carried out in mime.[8]]

---

8. *Liberation of the Actor*, p. 30.

CHAPTER 3

The Art of Listening

Forms of Listening

We have tried to observe how a speaker arrives at speaking a word or sentence. We now turn our attention to the speaker's partner—that is, to the person who is listening. The quality of a conversation depends in large measure on what takes place in the person to whom words are directed. In the extreme case, which is not uncommon in certain phases of a conversation, several people speak at the same time; also, people speak "at each other." Sometimes this is not even experienced as disturbing, for example, when under the influence of alcohol. Often we experience a temporary power struggle to see who will give in first and let the other speak. However, simply not speaking does not necessarily mean that a person is really listening. Often, while others are speaking, we can observe ourselves drifting off, having new insights, fixating on a word that was spoken and then associating our own experiences to it. Perhaps we also allow ourselves to be distracted by elements from other sensory realms. Interesting thought and image complexes can be developed from the hairstyle, rings, or jacket our partner may be wearing. The picture hanging on the wall opposite us, the dishes in the display case, the sugar bowl—all of these can stimulate us to the most varied sequences of pictures imaginable. Sometimes, awakening from these picture "excursions," we even feel a little ashamed that we have not been giving our full attention to the other person.

Then we really begin to pay attention to what the other person is saying. We concentrate entirely on the content. In doing so, we realize that we often understand what the other person is saying long before he or she has finished speaking. This is one of the reasons why we often interrupt so impolitely. Another is that we may be deeply engaged in the topic under discussion. In this case, we wander less but we still listen one-sidedly. Our listening is directed only toward the content and not enough toward our partner. This is the way an official interrogator looking for a mistake would listen to a suspect. Or a curious matchmaker might listen in this way to find out another's secrets. Undoubtedly, both my interest in the subject and my interest in my speaking partner increase my attention. Depending upon which is stronger, my listening will be more related to the information or to my partner. What is usually not taken in with full consciousness is the how—the form of language used, the choice of words, and, above all, the tone of voice.

We usually only react when the tone of voice is calculated to have effect. For example, a mother asks her fourteen-year-old daughter to clean up her room. The mother says, "You could still clean up your room!" The daughter replies, "Yes." The mother then perceives so much resistance and rejection in this "yes" that she says, "There is no need to act this way. I am really leaving you free." To which the daughter answers, "I said, yes, I will do it!" The entire conversation here lives in the tension between the form and content. In reality, the daughter's "yes" says: "It sucks! I have other things planned, your words irritate me," and so on. Those are the (unspoken) words the mother is reacting to, not to the argument implied by the word "yes." But the daughter's tone cancels the agreement implied by the content of her "yes" and thereby dialectically confuses the actual response. Such conversations are quite common in daily life. We must bear in mind that tone of voice and all other sense-perceptible elements (mimicry, gesture, and so on) affect the conversation partner even if not intended to do so by the speaker. Precisely because in this age of information, we are so fixated on the content of conversation we are inclined to overestimate the realm of meaning and to neglect other sense-perceptible elements. Stated in an extreme form: *We tend to want to understand before we have actually listened.* But, let us remember that, as children, we would never have begun speaking had we not first listened and then spoken what we had heard *only after understanding it.* A young child reacts almost exclusively to the voice in which something is said. Meaning is conveyed simultaneously by the sound of the voice, the rhythm, and the melody.

The Varied Effects of Speech Elements on the Listener

The social effects of language are existential and direct. This becomes clear when we pay attention to the way in which we hear speech. If we listen to how wind blows through leaves on a tree or hear a bell ringing, the sizzle of a grill, or the impact of a hammer blow, we can notice how hearing these sounds is fundamentally different from listening to human speech. Compared to human speech, these sounds are somehow "external," lacking an "inside." Language not only stimulates the process of hearing but also initiates a movement beyond what is heard. We can see this movement in the larynx. When listening to someone speak, we quietly imitate their speech movements with our own larynx. Occasionally, when the speaker stutters, or his or her voice is hoarse or is in some other way impaired, we can become conscious of this fact. Listening then becomes torture, because we ourselves experience the speaker's struggle to bring forth words. If a speaker is hoarse and has to constantly clear his or her throat, then the sound of throat clearing can soon be heard throughout the room.

The sense-perceptible elements already mentioned are also very important when it comes to recognizing dialects. A foreign language that we do not know can convey a great deal to us—even when we do not understand its meaning—if we open ourselves to its sound. Experiments have shown that infants can distinguish between language and other acoustical impressions. Once we have discovered this aspect of language, which we otherwise know only from poetry, entirely new worlds open up for us. We realize that we are constantly being formed and influenced by our partner in conversation, entirely independently of the content of what is being spoken.

This influence centers, above all, on our breathing. Our breathing reacts to the speaker in very subtle ways. A speaker who is short of breath makes us short of breath; one who speaks calmly, calms us. We react very sensitively to the various qualities of the human voice. There are people who accentuate everything sharply, nailing down each and every syllable, so to speak; others speak constantly in the same tone of voice without articulation; still others speak melodically, alternating between high and low. One voice attacks us, and we instinctively defend ourselves against it; a second voice puts us to sleep; while a third sweeps us along. There are whiny, flattering, and wobbly voices; voices ruled by vowels or consonants. Some people always speak as though they were offended, as if they had just been reprimanded. Others are bursting with self-confidence.

The Voice

I am not speaking here of the way a voice may adapt to a particular situation, but rather of the fundamental hue or tone with which everything is said, independent of its content. Through their mother-tongue, temperament, and character all human beings possess their own particular vocal characteristics with which they influence their partners' breathing and mood. When we realize this, we become conscious of our social responsibility when speaking. We can recognize in ourselves the sympathetic or antipathetic, pleasant or unpleasant feelings called forth by our partner's voice. We also must admit to the effect our voice has on others. This is reflected in the German language by the relationship between the word for voice, *Stimme,* and the word for mood, *Stimmung.* Training in conversation means acquiring the ability to use our voice in a way that is appropriate to both theme and partner.

Because the effects of a person's voice are less clearly perceived than the content of his or her speech, it often does not occur to a group that some participants in a conversation have difficulty influencing the conversation, even though the content of their contributions may be quite good. The reason for this could be an obnoxious tone of voice. In addition to the fundamental tone or hue of a person's voice, skilled listening will detect a speaker's present state. We can recognize whether the partner is excited, inhibited, uncertain, or hesitant. A mother listens to her child's voice to determine whether something is wrong or not right in what the child is saying. This is something in addition to the tone of voice appropriate to the subject and habitual tone fundamental to the child. Here a world opens itself to the listener and reveals its entire richness independent of the ideas under discussion. But, beyond these voice characteristics that exert a determining effect on the conversation, we come to a central mystery which can, through careful listening, reveal itself to us immediately. This is the fact that the unmistakable uniqueness of the speaker is revealed in the sense world. Just as everyone has his or her own face, so too everyone has his or her own voice, by which they can be identified, and seen, and understood.

Active, Selfless Listening

If we concentrate our hearing until we are filled with the sound of another's voice, then an intimate encounter with the essence of the speaker can come about. Mediated through listening we become aware of a "foreign" *I-ness*. In his unfinished book *Anthroposophy (A Fragment)*, Rudolf Steiner wrote:

Arriving at the conclusion that a human being is speaking seems simple to an unsophisticated mind, but in fact it is the result of very complicated processes. These processes all lead up to perceiving, in a sound in which one experiences oneself, another I at the same time. During this experience, everything else is disregarded; inasmuch as we turn our attention to it, the connection from I to I is what is

taken into account. The whole mystery of the empathy with the I of another is expressed in this fact,
a mystery we cannot attempt to describe other than
to say that we feel our own I in that of the other. If
we then perceive a sound coming from the other I,
our own I lives in that sound and therefore in the
other I.[1]

In actual life this condition can be maintained only
for a very short time. Our consciousness is distracted almost immediately by other elements, such as the context, our own thoughts, and so on. To maintain this
state requires of listeners the conscious will to devote
themselves entirely to what is heard. Because in this
state one's consciousness is with the other person, not
with oneself, this state is actually nothing other than
selflessness in the true sense of the word: I must completely extinguish my own sense of self to allow only
what comes from the other person to be present in me.
This is seldom achieved. It requires me to put aside for
a moment the whole jumble of my own thoughts, images, feelings, bodily sensations, and so forth. But the
moment I become conscious of my perception of the
other, I am already no longer in the state of selflessness.
I therefore pull myself together again and try to forget
myself; then I awake in myself again. The process is one
of falling asleep and awakening—but in this case falling
asleep is brought about by a conscious act of will.

To truly listen means, then, to fall asleep, to forget
oneself, even to lose a part of oneself. But, when we
understand—and even more importantly, make judg-

---

1. Rudolf Steiner, *Anthroposophy (A Fragment)* (Hudson, NY: Anthroposophic Press, 1996).

ments—we awaken. Wakeful consciousness arises as we separate ourselves from our surroundings. Inasmuch as I can distinguish myself from the things around me, I am awake; when I give myself to the world around me, I am asleep to myself. To listen in a conversation means to unite oneself with the other person; but organizing what has been heard and speaking means asserting oneself.

Every genuine conversation that lives in such a rhythm of sleeping and waking becomes an archetype of social life. But if it remains superficial and on the level of mere intellectual understanding—if only content is exchanged and the participants stay with arguments—then they will not come any closer to each other. Otto Friedrich Bollow remarked: "When I feel I need to prove something, then I am no longer speaking with the other person."[2] Speaking out of a real listening and perceiving of the other person enables a true encounter to occur, from which new possibilities can arise. The way we listen enables others to speak. In other words, to actively listen means giving others the possibility of saying things that they could not otherwise have said—or could not have said in the same way.

Because listening is usually given the least amount of attention, I have placed it in the foreground. But other realms of perception involved in a conversation—eyes, gestures, facial expressions—could have served just as well to reveal a conversation's deeper aspects.

Conversational Exercises

2. Otto Friedrich Bollow, *Sprache und Erziehung*, Stuttgart, 1966, p. 38.

Spiritual-Mindfulness

This German word *Geistesgegenwart* (the original name for this exercise) is very difficult to translate and means, literally, "spiritual presence." The English phrase, *presence of mind*, does not quite do it justice. *Spiritual presence* is a soul capacity that enables one to do or say the right thing at the right time—that is, *mindfulness.* Spiritual-mindfulness exercises focus on heightening the ability to take an active part in the process of conversation—that is, the ability to be actively present. This applies both to speaking in a way appropriate to the phase of conversation and appropriate to the theme being developed. Again, we work in a circle.

- Right listening, or *right silence.* One tries to perceive the *speaker,* the individual, not just the appearance. With thorough attentiveness, one tries not to allow one's own thoughts (criticism, response, and so on) but tries to "step into" the thoughts of the speaker. Occasionally consider whether or not one has understood the speaker.

- Try to perceive the speaker with one's feeling. Try to *silence* one's own sympathy and antipathy. One is not trying to gauge feelings *about* the speaker but is trying to *feel cognitively* the other individual. Interest may be artificial at first, but this will dissolve as one releases tensions, which is the real exercise. To release such tensions, one could imagine the appropriate gesture for listening, such as a feather carried on a breeze—lightly, with no resistance.

- When speaking, even in a group, one is speaking to individuals. As with listening, one considers who the other is and tries to stimulate interested understanding in the listener. Awareness is directed toward the other in both speaking and listening.[3]

3. Publisher's note: These suggestions were adapted from Georg Kühlewind, *From Normal to Healthy: Paths to the Liberation of Consciousness* (Hudson, NY: Lindisfarne Press, 1988). For further reading, see especially the section "Speaking and Listening," pp. 97–107.

CHAPTER 4

Stages of Conversation

Spontaneous Conversation

The character of a conversation depends upon the consciousness with which it is conducted. Spontaneous, everyday conversation requires the least spiritual and mental effort. Little thought precedes individual contributions; we follow whatever occurs to us spontaneously and react in an unpremeditated manner. Such conversations occur in restaurants, on street corners, at home around the dinner table, at hair salons, and so on. They arise within, and result from, a spontaneous situation for which no one has prepared. At most, perhaps the external framework for the conversation has been arranged: the in-laws have been invited to dinner, or the Smith family is being visited at their new home. What is decisive is that the conversation simply arises through the situation. People meet and a conversation results from the encounter.

But how, in fact, do our contributions to a conversation arise if we are really only yielding to spontaneous impulses? Let us imagine that our parents have invited us on a beautiful summer evening to a family festival and that they set before us a freshly baked, homemade pizza. Our joyous "Ah!" is followed by various sequences of inner images. Perhaps the daughter remembers that six months earlier, when she ate pizza at the Millers' house,

that pizza was bought. Because of a misunderstanding,
Mr. Miller was late, upsetting his wife—and so on. The
brother, however, experiences something quite different. He thinks, "But there is much too much cheese on
it! Watch out! Stomach ache! The doctor warned me
only last week. And I haven't even paid his last bill. I
really must have a raise." His wife, on the other hand,
thinks of Florence as soon as she sees the pizza. "We
were there at Easter. We always ate pizza, at noon, on
the Cathedral square. There was a nice waiter. This
year, we haven't planned anything yet for summer vacation." Everyone around the table similarly experiences
a sequence of thoughts and mental images. The course
of the conversation is thus determined as the participants choose any of these images and toss them into
the conversation. The daughter, for example, may ask
after the Millers. The brother might speak about the
injustice of the pay scale, while his wife asks her
brother-in-law where he vacations. All these contributions appear to be without connection even though, in
fact, they all began with the pizza. Everyone has such
associations but they are all different. If we follow this
uncontrolled, inner production of mental images we
create a conversation with a constantly changing theme
that always remains on the surface. Of course, other
people's contributions also provide material for association. Observing ourselves, we can note how ideas and
images—some of them based only on sound—are
attached to individual words heard in the conversation.
When someone mentions a possible stomach pain or
"cramp," caused by jogging too soon after pizza,
another person may comment on how the car was too
crowded on the ride over, and they really do need a
larger vehicle. Such examples show how egotistic this

form of conversation can be. Here is an extreme example: Someone returns from vacation and wants to tell others about his experiences. Right after he mentions the location, his conversational partner remembers the time he was there and immediately begins to tell of his experiences without allowing the other to say a word. The advantage of such conversations is the casualness that permits uncomplicated conversational contact between partners.

If we ask ourselves what law the various associations are following, we come to the life of feelings. Those mental pictures with which we are united most strongly will rise into our consciousness most readily. Anyone who has just had a significant experience, or is about to have one—an examination, a wedding, or a painful insult—can experience how the sequence of associated pictures unfolds in so refined a manner that it inevitably steers consciousness toward the experienced or anticipated event. Even when we are engaged in focused study, a word we have read can set off a sequence of images in our mind that inevitably leads to the event. There seems to be a force that is powerfully influenced by what is emotionally important to us and works like a magnetic field in our half-conscious mind. Whatever lies closest to our feelings forces itself into our consciousness by attaching itself to our perceptions.

Conversations situated in feelings and sense perception in this way are full of life. We are warmed by them without having to exert any effort. It is difficult to organize such a conversation because the entire surrounding field of the senses exerts such a powerful influence. We can only observe a beginning phase of gradual warming and then the rhythmical ebb and flow of contributions from various participants. Phases of the conversation, during which several people speak at the same time, come and go. Pauses in such a conversation are difficult to bear. People become uncomfortable when no one is speaking. The moment of embarrassment, in which many possible topics are considered, ends only when the apple pie—or some other *deus ex machina*—is brought and supplies the solution. Warmth and satisfaction arise through the fact of conversation, not through its content. Each partner's "You" is perceived through feelings that arise in hearing and seeing the other. When leaving such an encounter one does not say, "That was an interesting conversation!" but rather, "It was nice to see you again." In such a case it would have been entirely out of place to admonish one's partner to stick to the point. The casual jumping around from topic to topic—expressions of spontaneous insights—properly belongs in this kind of conversation.

Linguistically, such conversations are characterized by numerous exclamations and a full spectrum of sounds. We can see how strongly contributions are related to feelings and the speaker's I, if we note the typical sequence of subject and object in spontaneous conversations. Here are two actual sentences: "Wow, its so clear, this crystal!" The predicate follows the expression of feeling; the subject appears first as a pronoun, "it"; and only at the conclusion becomes a substantive noun. The speaker begins with what is closest to him or her and gradually finds the path to the listener, "Whew! Did you notice how fast it went by, this last week?" The listener hears first an expression of feeling "Whew!"; then the question concerning something he or she knows nothing about, "did you also notice"; then about a fast moving something, "how fast it went by"; and then, finally, "this last week." Logic would require the reverse sequence. First the listener should know the theme under discussion (this last week), then discover what is predicated—that is, what's actually being said about the theme—and then the question about agreement. But such a logical sequence would signify a distance from what is being expressed, while the authentic form conveys the emotional connection.

The form of conversation we have described is a tendency that never appears to the total exclusion of all other conversational forms, because even in a spontaneous conversation a human being does not consist only of feelings. Sometimes a participant is allowed to consciously pursue an idea for as long as he or she wants; speakers generally remain on a topic only for a short time. My purpose here is merely to point out the connection between soul life and the form of a conversation. In other words, a spontaneous conversation is interesting, not because of its content but because of its psychology.

Any education in the art of conversation must know about these processes, because tendencies that are entirely natural and justified in spontaneous everyday conversations can have a devastating effect on conversations intended to achieve insight or to arrive at a collective decision. In the latter, spontaneous tendencies need to be overcome or directed.

Intentional, guided conversation

We begin with the form of conversation in which the leaders and the led are assigned fixed roles, by considering conversations intended to achieve insight or to arrive at decision. Here one conversational partner more or less forces the others into certain paths or "tracks." An extreme example of this is interrogation. In this case, the interrogator forces the individual being interrogated to answer with some content that is already fixed. All attempts at distraction are immediately suppressed. A milder form of interrogation is the examination. Here there is also clearly one who leads and those who follow. Nevertheless, we know that a certain ability in psychology combined with the necessary chutzpah can enable some examinees to guide or steer their examiners.

The next step in this process is the teaching conversation. The teacher clearly steers the process and expects the pupil to move within preestablished boundaries. Thus the teacher can convey material in a more interesting way than simply by lecturing. He or she can also test existing knowledge and thereby foster the learning process. We have become so accustomed to this assignment of roles that we easily overlook its one-sidedness. When the teacher asks the class, "Now, what did we discuss yesterday?" he or she ought to be surprised that no one responds by saying, "Don't you remember?" This one-sidedness has a special effect in higher grades when an apparently free conversation is simulated, yet the results are inevitably what the teacher planned at the outset.

We must understand the difference between a skilled and an unskilled conversational leader. Both kinds can work within an accepted or institutionalized authoritarian relationship. One determines the conversation completely and uses the contributions from others only to serve his or her own purpose. Good conversational leaders, however, place themselves at the service of the conversation, so that it unfolds in an orderly fashion and no participant is suppressed or allowed to dominate. A good conversational leader may be compared to a conductor who serves the piece being performed and uses the perceptions of the orchestra members to achieve a joint creation with all involved. The opposite would be a tyrannical conductor who subjects everything to his or her own will.

It is good to become aware of these forms in their purity because they can arise in every kind of conversation, usually with a negative effect. It is intolerable to be in a decision-making conversation among adults in which one of the participants, perhaps even the leader, either addresses others like a didactic village schoolmaster or willfully manipulates the proceedings like a demagogue.

The most beautiful examples of good teaching conversations in which the learning process is facilitated in an almost ideal fashion are Plato's dialogues. With great dialectical mastery, Socrates brings his conversational partners to the insight that they do not know, and hence to the possibility of truly knowing. Although, at the beginning, Socrates' partners may appear equal or superior to him in knowledge, nevertheless he always shows himself to be the true teacher who, through his competence, is sovereign in the field. Socrates can be forgiven his hidden, clever guidance because his pedagogical goal is to lead his partners to self-knowledge and thereby to independence. He acts not for himself, but for others.

Between Chaos and Rigidity

Let us now consider conversations that have no naturally assigned roles and yet, unlike spontaneous conversations, are organized both as to content and to order of discussion. Conferences with colleagues, discussions, discussion groups, studying a common text, colloquies, negotiations, and so on, are all of this type.

Every appearance of concentration on the theme and all efforts to organize the discussion indicate thoughtful reflection. This fact alone can already awaken distrust or even antipathy in some participants. Such people fear that spontaneity, freedom, and warmth will be lost. They see leadership in the conversation as burdensome or patronizing and consider raising of hands, for instance, or any other preliminary indication of one's desire to speak, to be artificial hindrances. A leader for them is totally unnecessary. "Don't we trust one another?" they say. They do not want to forego the advantages of a spontaneous conversation. To some extent, they have a point. A conference with a written protocol that contains time allotments for individual items, together with all the other usual organizational forms, can become austere and official in tone. Indeed, we have all experienced how nothing new arises in thoroughly organized and strictly conducted conversations. The anticipated items unfold in the ritual form already provided. This phenomenon is connected with the kind of human thinking fundamental to every organization. This kind of thinking, which could be called intellectual (German, *verständing*), is oriented essentially by the past. A question is analyzed and structured for the conversation on the basis of past experience. If the question allows the planned path through the conversation to be followed, it is judged to be good. If, however, complications and new questions arise, the preparation is considered to have been inadequate. Intellect in this sense also addresses itself to the realm of things and rejects anything personal. Conversation dominated by the intellect is therefore exactly the opposite of spontaneous conversation.

If the crusaders for the intellect and logic emerge victorious in a group, then the conversation does not, as a rule, last as long. No one really gets very warm, and the participants become less and less active. No good insights occur, or if they do, fear suppresses them. On the other hand, if the critics of this approach prevail, then the conversations last for a long time, and if decisions are made, they often remain unclear, and everyone interprets them in their own way. The result is that, by, the next conversation, everyone has forgotten them, since no one kept notes. In conversations shaped by intellect and logic, personal colors recede into the background, but personal tensions are unavoidable when such a conversation is waylaid by critics who step forward and push their point of view with extreme one-sidedness.

Thus, we have become acquainted with the two possible forms of one-sidedness in conversation: on one side, luxuriant chaotic growth, the danger that everything becomes mushy, with too little structure, and ultimately, inconsequential outcome; on the other hand, we find the danger that the organization suffocates insight to the extent that participants and their qualities can no longer influence the conversation. Chaos and rigidity are both enemies of lively conversation.

Hence the question: How can we lead a conversation in such a way that we neither lose the positive qualities of a spontaneous conversation nor introduce uncontrolled elements? This question could also be asked the other way around. How can one organize a conversation without losing its objective efficiency, but so that as many people as possible can bring as much of themselves as they can into it? The technique known as "brainstorming" arose out of the experience of this kind of conversation. Brainstorming in this sense is an early phase of conversation in which everyone freely expresses whatever occurs to them in response to the question at hand. Often a kernel of gold can be found under the verbiage of this process.

Once again, let me stress that some form of organization is necessary as soon as we go beyond a simple exchange of information—that is, conversation. Otherwise, because of personal friction and lack of form, the loss is too great.

The Ideal Form

I would now like to illuminate the question from another side. As we have seen, the intellect is based on what has already become the past. When used as a means to organize, this leads to routine. However, in a conversation convened to arrive at decisions based on knowledge, just the opposite is needed—we want something new and unforeseen to arise. How, then, do we move from thinking determined by the past to presence of mind, the present where spiritual insights can enter our minds? We experience the present intensely in spontaneous conversation. But we experience it through feelings and emotions stimulated by the senses, by images from the sense world, and not through true presence of mind, or spiritual insight.

Certainly it can be an advance if we can suppress negative elements through forms of organization. But can't we move beyond old forms to arrive at new forms? Can't we regard all our preparatory work as a preliminary aid, to be dispensed with when we no longer need it? This approach would be similar to that taken by a teacher who carefully prepares a lesson, yet is prepared to modify or even drop it if the actual teaching situation requires it. This assumes a special sensitivity to what lives in the present. We must perceive the circumstances, the situation, the individual participants as well as their contributions. The ideal is to act out of the situation as it presents itself in the moment without losing sight of the goal.

Doing this is a question of attitude and intention. We can see this clearly if we compare a conversation ruled by contradiction to a conversation truly concerned with acquiring insight. In the former, the participants in the conversation believe that they must win the others over to their own viewpoint in the course of the conversation. For this reason, participants take advantage and strengthen their own position by seeking out every weakness in their partners, every gap in their arguments, and every unclear formulation. They listen to the others' words only to discover what might be useful for a counterargument. This process does not facilitate learning—at most, it hones the participants' skill in dialectic. Conversations of this kind are not concerned with who is right, but only with who has the better arguments. That is why there is often a winner and loser at the end, unless, of course, arguments are simply repeated endlessly, as is often the case with teenagers. Anyone who departs from the original position in such a conversation has lost face, and therefore the debate. The only pleasure to be found here lies in the sparkling intelligence of argument. But this pleasure is often only the seductive pleasure of one's own cleverness at the expense of others.

Everything is quite different in a conversation genuinely aimed at achieving insight. Here, too, the play of dialectic and imagination governs the conversation, but now it is in the service of the search for truth. There is a common goal: greater knowledge. Therefore there are no losers. In this case, questions, objections, and provocations have only one purpose—to highlight the subject under discussion and to further the development of thought. The fundamental attitude is that of a question addressed to the truth—to be unveiled and developed gradually so that, in the end, it is revealed equally to everyone. Of course, this presupposes that the participants enter fully into the thinking process, helping it along through their contributions, so that something hidden can be brought to conscious insight and lifted into the realm of knowledge for everyone present. Imagine a conversation in which everyone begins with this attitude of truth-seeking, in which every contribution is carefully taken up and weighed to discern what further questions and contributions appropriately connect with what has just been said, thereby giving the whole group thought-process an opportunity to further unfold. When this happens, we enter a realm where conversation becomes art.

Conversational Exercises

Word games

- One person begins by saying a word, and the next must say a word rhyming with the first before going on to a new word.

- One person begins with a word; the next must say the first word backward before going on to a new word.

- Going around a circle, we create phrases or sentences using words with first a growing, then a diminishing, number of syllables. For example, *a creaking wobbly intricately constructed wagon wheel.*[1]

---

1. For a rich treasure trove of word games see Paul Matthews, *Sing Me the Creation.*

CHAPTER 5

Conversation as an Art

What are the elements of an artistic process? On the one hand, we have the material means of expression: color, form, tone, sound, and so forth. On the other, there is the impulse to shape, that impels the artist to bring the material into a specific form. The artistic imagination works in both spheres, mediating between matter and form. It seeks to imprint matter so that the impulse to form can appear in the realm of the senses as completely as possible. Thus two sources stimulate the imagination: the sense world from which the means of art arise and the world of inspiration that appears in the soul of the artist as the will to form. Following Schiller, we could say that a work of art comes about when an artist enters into a "playful" relationship with both the material-sensible and the supersensible worlds. When artists do this they are free; otherwise they are subject, as Schiller says, to the necessities of either the senses or reason.

What does all this mean for conversation? To begin with, we can easily recognize in Schiller's two coercions the two forms of one-sidedness possible in a conversation: the necessary predominance of the senses in spontaneous conversation and, in organized conversation, the dominance of a logical compulsion.

This poses some questions: What elements of a conversation correspond to the sense realm? Where are the sources of inspiration? What constitutes the play of imagination? We must bear in mind that several people work together in conversation. Hence, we find models for conversation among the classical arts: music (especially in the performance of existing works), theater, and dance. A great difference, of course, between conversation and the arts is the fact that artists usually work with predetermined materials such as musical notes, choreography, texts, and so on.

A preliminary answer to these questions is found in chapter 3. The element to be shaped and formed is found in everything that our listening can give us. To this we must add our perception of nonverbal expressions. Listening presents me with the thoughts, feelings, intentions, and moods of the others. From the perception of these, I receive insights and themes that I then bring into the flow of conversation. Imagination consists of *whether*, *when*, and *how* I put what I understand into words, based on what I have heard. Yet, isn't listening itself also a formative element? Am I not actively intervening through the very fact that I am listening, and even more through the way in which I listen? Undoubtedly! Imagination in conversation is found in our freedom to play between listening, developing thoughts, and formulating contributions—between "falling asleep" to ourselves and listening to others, and "awakening" to ourselves and speaking.

Play consists in the search for balance between various polar elements. This is what Ruth Cohn had in mind in her outstanding contributions to a modern training in conversation, when she speaks of having to find the balance between three major elements: the theme (it), one's own self (I) and the group (We).[1] As soon as one of these elements is overly dominant or neglected, something must be done to reestablish a balance. Since the situation is not static and given, but always changing in the dynamic course of the conversation, constant, spiritual presence of mind is required. It is this presence of mind that allows me to act out of momentary perception creatively.

A conversation unfolds in time. Therefore, to understand a conversation's artistic elements, we must concern ourselves with the form of a conversation as it changes through time. Conversation is related in this way to other artistic forms such as music, poetry, and dance, and requires time to unfold. If we consider only an individual sentence or word, we can already see that the temporal sequence is decisive. We recognize "door" or "road" from the sequence of sounds that make up these words. The sequence of every sentence signifies a whole. But this whole has a different character for every different sequence. The same is true of conversations. The same words can have entirely different meaning according to the momentary situation. Many of us have experienced how a conversational contribution can disappear into empty space without a response from anyone present, but how an hour later the same contribution from the same speaker, now reformulated, achieves a powerful effect. "Yes! Of course. We must do that!" is now the reaction.

---

1. Ruth Cohn, *Von der Psychoanalyse zur themenzentrierten Interaktion*, Stuttgart, 1975.

The same is true of a piece of music. We cannot change the sequence of notes without changing the notes themselves, because now they are in a different context. In music, just as in conversation, the elements that have gone before must be carefully considered and woven into the present as a determining factor. That is, we must see conversation as time that has been shaped and given contours.

Conversation as Shaped Time

Flowing water is the most beautiful picture for the passing flow of time. Language itself directs us to this connection between conversation and the mobility of all that is fluid in nature. It follows a "course," it "flows," it "streams," it can be "blocked," it can "bubble," sometimes it "overflows its banks," it can be "deep" or "dry"— almost all are pictures of moving water. For this reason, we will acquire a foundation for our observations of conversation by investigating the elements of flowing water.

A river constantly needs new material (water) both from its source and from its tributaries; otherwise, it will dry up. A conversation also needs substance in the form of contributions that are basic, nourishing, and advance or promote the theme. The slope of a river from its origins down to the ocean gives it a movement that leads it downhill to the river's mouth. Conversations also live through movement and must likewise flow forward. The interaction between the riverbed— whether stone, sand, or earth—and the flowing water creates tension. Rocky hindrances such as canyons create narrow passages that give way to flatter terrain. A conversation similarly only gets going, starts to move, when some kind of tension is present. The tension between the experience of *not-knowing* and our faith in the partner who *knows* creates a question. Objections and contradictions keep the conversation alive. Conversations are very hard to start when no differences— ideological or personal—are experienced. Finally, a fourth element can be observed in the river: its direction. It is well known that water never flows straight. Water naturally wants to meander rhythmically in and out of the central axis of the river's flow, and, if it does not dry up, it will continue to flow toward the lower-lying estuary or mouth. A conversation also moves in a direction, toward an end. It has a direction and a goal toward which it strives, whether expressed or not.

We have found four elements that determine the course of a conversation, and we will now consider these more closely. Like a river, a conversation has substance, it has tempo or pace, tension, and also direction—all interdependent. It is easy to see that the volume of water, the slope, and the size of the riverbed are connected and together determine the direction. The separation of these into individual elements is only necessary for a preliminary understanding.

a) Substance

To begin with, substance means "theme." Conversation must flow in *something*. But substance also means the substantive individual contributions. We must ask the question: Is there enough material for a fruitful conversation or perhaps too much, some of which we simply cannot master? Depending upon the goal of the conversation we must judge whether we are all addressing the same theme. This question should be asked particularly at the beginning of a conversation and be combined with another question: Does everyone have the same foundation—that is, has everyone informed themselves concerning the theme so that they are in a position to contribute to the conversation. The first phase often only consists of this: conveying to those present the knowledge necessary to converse intelligently.

The rest of the conversation has to do with assuring that a healthy relationship arises between the wealth of material and its processing by the individual contributions. Because the whole conversation is a process unfolding in time, this relationship is very unstable, falling off balance with each new contribution. Therefore, the task arises anew every moment—depending on the momentary state of balance—either to seek a renewal of the material or to try to limit it. We need a wealth of insight and imagination to renew the material, while to "reign it in," or limit a conversation, we need a willingness to limit ourselves, a capacity for renunciation. We must distinguish between the quantity and the quality of the material in doing either of these. There are people who have continuous insights but no real depth; and others who rarely speak, but often create real substance with their contributions. There are those who are talkative and those who are mostly silent, and often wise. Hence, on the level of substance we can recognize a twofold task: on the one hand, to renew through imagination; and, on the other, to limit and make depth possible.

b) Pace and Flow

Many of us may have experienced committee meetings in which the chair makes a suggestion, and then immediately goes on to say, "Is anyone against it? No? Good, then it is decided!" Some of the participants may be quietly thinking that the process might have proceeded a little too fast, but hesitate to make themselves unpopular by speaking up and saying that the speed at which the meeting is moving is interfering with conversation. A similar degree of discomfort can be felt when deliberations over fundamental principles focus endlessly on points that are really only quite minor—with the result that no time is left for the main issues. We can also observe that a conversation does not need to proceed at a steady pace but may be accelerated or slowed down. In the same way, we can become sensitive to whether the conversation needs to be accelerated or slowed in any particular phase.

There is a natural speed curve. A conversation whose function is to acquire insight or arrive at a decision usually unfolds slowly while the participants fully engage with the material; once this has happened, it accelerates as questions and insights start flowing; and then it slows down again as the material is used up or the time allotted comes to an end. We can see from this how pace is related to the amount of material.

Individual contributions can either speed up or slow down. If, for example, someone says that everyone present should speak out about a given question, then a slowing down will occur. But if someone says, "Remember, there are ten points on today's agenda," then the pace definitely picks up, assuming, of course, that this contribution is accepted by the others.

An individual participant's relationship to the theme will also determine whether his or her contribution is intended to speed up or slow the pace. Those who make new suggestions or bring forward new initiatives will naturally want to accelerate the conversation; they are convinced of the necessity of their suggestions, and to attain their end, feel they must only deal with this and eliminate any objections from others. But those who have to evaluate these suggestions need time to ask questions, and may have objections. In other words, they hinder the decision. It is the bitter but necessary experience of the fiery member of a group that for an initiative to become the common decision of all, it must first be cooled in the reflective thought of others. We need the driving will-element of participants with initiative, but we also need the retarding forces of the prudent, who hesitate. Those who hold back liberate the initiators from their egocentricity and thereby bind them into the community.

Additionally, there are participants whose fundamental character accelerates the conversation, and others who apply the brakes to it. The first group includes the pragmatists and realists; the second, the theoreticians and fundamentalists.

In a conversation the pragmatists and realists seek to discover the practicality of the given circumstances, while the theoreticians and fundamentalists want to examine carefully all the questions of principle involved. It is easy to see that this can greatly delay, if not altogether block a decision. For this reason, anyone who consciously desires to impede a decision will, for rhetorical reasons, raise the question of basic principles.

When considering the allotment of time—that is, the shaping of time available to us—we need to distinguish between purely external and internal time.

Breaks, for example, are an essential element that, while working externally to hinder and slow the process, inwardly accelerate it. Externally, a break means absence from deliberations. Inwardly, however, breaks make it possible to absorb what has already been said and prepare new initiatives for discussion. Becoming competent in conversation means, among other things, developing a sense for the moment when a conversation should be interrupted, when a preliminary end has been reached. We all know what can happen if this is not noticed; the fruits of conversation that could have been harvested are easily lost by talking them into the ground. Everything said about active listening also applies to breaks. Every impulse must have a chance to fade away like an echo, must be taken into sleep, so to speak. It is also a question of tact not to respond immediately to certain kinds of contributions, such as personal confessions.

c) Tension

Human beings have an entirely natural tendency to respond to any viewpoint, with the opposite point of view. This is also true in conversation. A tendency to contradict arises within a discussion group that has reached agreement on a matter, not because we are really of a different opinion, but to set something against the mood of unison. We cannot achieve real knowledge without this principle of contradiction. The dialectical element, the tentative consideration of the most varied possibilities, accompanies every genuine act of judgment. In conversation, this process is distributed among the various participants and creates the necessary tension. Every contribution is highlighted by a response. Of course, the tension between different sides of an argument can easily be carried over to a tension between those representing them. If this happens, the conversation becomes emotional and progress becomes questionable. In addition to tension between the various points of view and arguments, there is also the tension between various groups of participants.

Every question, aside from mere contradiction and objection, introduces an element of tension that helps to clearly define the conversation. Answers, on the other hand, dissolve tensions and thereby work toward a conclusion. For this reason, questioning is one means by which conversation is fostered. Questioning expresses dissatisfaction with the present state of affairs and communicates hope for some future development for the better. When posed honestly, every question expresses a crisis, a dramatic element, without which one cannot arrive at insight or a common decision. Therefore, the more intensively questioning occurs, the richer the tension and the more fruitful a conversation can be. Later, we will explore the qualities of questions and discuss their significance for conversation.

In contrast to questions, exploratory reports, presentations, and introductory descriptions have a relaxing character that may be seen in their tendency to put people to sleep.

Among the partisans of tension we must also number the conversational "characters" who prefer to play the devil's advocate and ask critical questions. They represent the spirit of opposition; they can barely tolerate agreement. There are also those who delight in provoking others and pose extreme scenarios for discussion to provoke others into contradicting them. Sometimes they continue arguments ad absurdum.

Tension is resolved by conciliatory mediators—peaceful citizens who do not wish to lose their calm—as well as by humorists who can defuse a situation through a well-timed joke. Then there are those conversational partners who, at the right moment, can always find precisely the right words to lead a con-versation through a tense moment.

d) Direction and Goal

Except for spontaneous conversation, an unstated agreement guides conversation: Conversation must not flow in every direction that appears, but must unfold along more or less prescribed paths. It is extremely helpful if participants agree at the outset what the goals are to be. Will there be nothing more than a free exchange of ideas? Is a common opinion to be sought for? Or is an agreement or a decision to be reached? The goal that is set determines the course and character of the conversation. Much emotional tension arises from diverging concepts of this common goal. But such misconceptions can easily be avoided by clarification.

Again, we must find the middle ground between two extremes. If the conversation is never allowed out of its prescribed channel, it will have a very difficult time unfolding, because the atmosphere of freedom is missing. The free expression of opinion is jeopardized in conversations conducted too strictly, because the fear of not addressing the theme prevents contributions. Because of this fear, it is difficult for anything new to arise in such conversations. On the other hand, a conversation in which everyone follows only their own insights will rarely achieve a goal. We must always find the middle ground between the canal and the flood, between compulsion and arbitrariness. Location checks ("Where do we stand now?), summaries, and a clarifying survey of ground already covered are techniques that awaken our consciousness and help us to find the lost path. Including material remote from the topic, as well as a variety of individual contributions, provides the necessary breadth. These two elements (discipline and freedom) alternate in a certain rhythm. At first, we agree on the goal and method; then the conversation expands; then comes a location check, which draws everything together; and this is then followed by the next expansion.

A special form of expansion occurs when the conversation changes from an objective relationship to the theme to a personal relationship. Any personal tensions that may arise tend to lead away from the theme and become self-supporting. At such times a clarifying comment pointing out the original question often relaxes the situation and leads the conversation back to its original direction. This role or task is often taken on by the leader of the conversation although there are also genuine conversational "clarifiers"—or born committee leaders. They are the "schoolmasters" who constantly call for order and discipline.

Schematically, we can imagine these four configurations as follows:

Substance: Content of theme, foundational material

- If there is too little substance, is the material exhausted? If so, the task is to renew it.

- Is there is so much material that it cannot be mastered? If so, then limit it.

Pace: How fast is the conversation moving?

- Does it flow too slowly? If so, accelerate it.
- Does it flow too quickly? If so, slow it down.

Tension: Does the conversation appear too formed and structured?

- Does it have limited form and procedural shape? If so, shape it.
- Does it have too much form? Is the tension too great? If so, there is the task of relaxing it, of bringing life and substance.

Direction toward goal: Where is the conversation going?

- Is the conversation diverging from its goal, losing its path? If so, the task is to reestablish its direction.
- Is it held in too narrow a channel? If so, can you expand it?

It is clear from this brief survey that these areas are closely related. Indeed, they may even appear to be identical at first, because we are viewing the same thing from four different points of view. We may notice that the first and fourth aspects have a special relationship. Each is a question of greater fullness or greater limitation. In the first, we are concerned with the material of the conversation, whether there is too much or too little. In the fourth, we consider whether the material needs to be expanded or limited in relation to the intended direction. A similarly close relationship exists between the second and third points of view. At first, it appears that a faster pace leads to greater tension. But it may be that an objection assists the flow. This is quite possible. But a faster pace can also be the result of inadequate preparation. So an objection may also simply block the flow.

This fourfold approach shows its fruitfulness whenever people are involved in actively shaping time, not just in observing conversation. In its purest form, this appears in music, considered to be the pure art of time. Likewise, a teacher can also ask whether the teaching plan for the hour has too much, too little, or just enough material; whether it is proceeding at the proper pace; whether there is enough tension and relaxation, contraction and expansion; and whether it is proceeding naturally toward its goal. We can view a speech, an essay, a story, and especially a drama from this point of view. One can also reverse the situation and recognize that a conversation held for the purpose of making a decision or acquiring knowledge is also a process that corresponds to a play, with its inherent tensions.

Conversation as a Dramatic Process

After analyzing many conversations, I have discovered an apparent parallel between the five acts of classical drama and the course of a conversation. This should not astonish us, since drama is the unfolding of a plot reflected in dialogue. Likewise, conversation presents us with acts of speech or language that allow the seeds of a plot or sequence of actions to unfold in the give and take of dialogue with one's partners. Considering conversation in this way allows us to recognize an ideal form allowing for many variations and modifications. Of course, this ideal seldom appears with pure form, any more than a play does.

According to Aristotle's original theory, the ideal drama consists of five parts or acts. The first act presents the exposition. We get to know the people, the scene, and the situation. Thus we know what is at stake and the relationships between the protagonists. Anyone who does not pay attention during the first act will have difficulty understanding what follows. In the second act, we notice a definite acceleration. Opposites clash, the plot sharpens. The peak is achieved in the third act. Decisive scenes unfold at this stage. For example, in Schiller's *Mary Stuart*, it is then that we find the only scene in which the two queens, the chief protagonists, meet. At this point, comedy threatens to enter. Confusion and misunderstandings reach a climax. The fourth act then follows with a delay. The plot is moved to a secondary theater of action or—to put it another way—secondary characters step into the foreground. Finally, the fifth act brings the resolution. In a tragedy, the hero dies; in a comedy, the separated couple find each other. In any case, the problem is solved.

We can summarize this sequence: The plot gets going and sharpens while driving toward a peak, a crisis. A solution is then developed out of the crisis as a new stage of transformation. Here we see the origin of drama in the ancient Mysteries. The soul is to be led by fear and compassion, through the crisis, to purification.

In drama, we have the artistic formation of a course of action, and we can follow every step as a process in time. A process has a beginning, escalates, reaches a high point, lets up, and then comes to a halt: 1. *Beginning;*

2. *Intensification/enhancement*; 3. *High point*; 4. *Diminution*; 5. *End*. Or: Set out (1); accelerate (2); travel (3); slow down (4); and, finally, stop (5). We can also find this trajectory appropriately modified in the time-form of a conversation.

Conversation as a Reflection of a Drama in Five Acts

It is quite natural that before the search for consensus begins, a conversation directed toward making decisions or acquiring insight must begin by establishing common criteria for judgment. Facts must be clarified, positions explained, and opinions and information exchanged.

1. Act One—*Exposition*: The organization of individual intentions, insights, opinions, and the exposition of joint direction. The tension between these becomes apparent.

2. Act Two—*Intensification*: If a mood of agreement is too strongly present, we find the need to oppose. As a rule, sharper words are spoken now. We can feel that the situation is serious and moving toward a critical point. We can observe that the main tension is limited to two possibilities. Even when a hundred possibilities exist, the moment comes when only two contrary positions remain for discussion.

3. Act Three—*Peripeteia* or *Reversal*: Powerful forces are set in motion. These may lead to a stalemate or a blockade, or they may seek to bring about a judgment or decision.

4. Act Four—*Retardation* must enter: The will impulses pushing toward decision must be slowed by the reflective thought-element. A break, a continuation of the plenum conversation in the form of individual conversations, or a thorough recapitulation of foregoing contributions in light of stated goals can all be helpful at this stage. Perhaps someone will provide a mediating suggestion, or describe the subject from an entirely different perspective.

5. Act Five—*Resolution*: We have suffered the crisis. Out of the transformed positions, consensus can now arise. But this consensus does not represent a victory of one party over another, but always introduces something new into the group discussion.

Pathological Forms

Anyone with a feeling for the process of shaping time will notice even the simplest offenses that disturb or block the conversation process. To pose a question of fact or lay down fundamentally new criteria for decision-making during the decisive, final phase of conversation is to be "out of step with the time" in the deepest sense—such efforts at clarification belong at the beginning. Neither should anyone at this phase of conversation refer back to what was said at the beginning, saying, "That's what I suggested at the start of our conversation!" This statement betrays the fact that the speaker was not counting on a real, conversational process that might have allowed for something new to arise during the conversation. Even the constellations, or particular factions of participants, may have completely changed in the interim. On the other hand, those who offer suggestions aimed directly at a decision, prior to an agreement on basic criteria, also demonstrate an "untimeliness."

Disagreeable and antagonistic contributions presented in the first act are not worth getting upset about, since all of the viewpoints belong to the foundations of a conversation. They must be included but are not decisive at this time. It is possible to speak objectively only after everything has been put on the table for discussion. Experience shows that the worst consequences result from transgressions in *Act Three*. I have already pointed out the chief mistake committed at this point: forcing a decision. When this is done, the conversation is, in reality, truncated. At this stage, we must listen to those who would slow down the process, and recommend delaying the decision. If we don't do this, then sooner or later the entire problem will reappear on the agenda and we will have to start all over again, because the apparent consensus was not genuine. But it is just as wrong to lose patience in the third act—to "throw in the towel"—or to focus on personal considerations—"If that happens, then I am leaving." We must accept the crisis, even welcome it, because with it comes the possibility of real transformation. It is also true that the greatest wakefulness and concentration is necessary at this stage, since everything is in question—including, it often seems, one's very existence—and the front line attitudes and positions are in danger of hardening, which can lead to battlefield conditions.

In these situations, we can often observe that, after a discussion, individuals tend to congregate with other like-minded participants in order to express their anger or irritation. We can well understand this need to comfort and strengthen one another; however, it can also poison the ongoing process. At this point in the process, individual conversations are meaningful only if they help to clarify the positions of opposing participants. New possibilities appear only when the front lines of the two warring factions are dissolved, but this means that opposing views cannot remain in opposition. Therefore here we need the ability to forego intransigent positions and to sacrifice rigid principles, which requires a pause or a break for self-reflection. Those who eventually come to different convictions than those held at the beginning do not lose face, but prove in this way that they have taken the decision-making process seriously, and thus have achieved something new.

A Temporally Justified Decision

After wrestling with a difficult theme, we can sometimes feel a definite decision floating in the air. If we go past the appropriate moment to "pluck the fruit," then it will rot. If we continue to speak, mixing additional new problems in with the old, we shall lose the moment of grace. Just as unripe fruit, ripped too soon from the tree, is inedible, overripe fruit is also not fit to eat. An artist in conversation needs an organ of perception to sense the *time-ripeness* of a problem. This is not only true for a decision, but for the entire process. The most varied factors must be considered and weighed: the time of day, the particular constellations of people present, the contributions already presented, the mood in the room. These aspects all present certain possibilities or moments when something is due. If the possibilities are not perceived, then the opportunity passes unused.

We can sense not only the appropriate moment, but also whose moment or turn has come. This is exemplified in the process of plucking the fruit of decision. It is a matter of tact and technique to arrange things so that the one who says, "I think we should do it this way!" is not the one who proposed the original idea and secretly thinks, "Finally, the others have also understood!" It is far more appropriate that the person who brought up the greatest objections also formulate and present the appropriate decision to the others. Whenever there are winners and losers, it is not art that rules, but power.

Simultaneity in Art

Every artist, and in fact anyone who enjoys art, faces the task of seeing numerous elements and factors working together at the same time—elements that may seem quite contradictory when viewed apart. For example, when listening to a string quartet we can analyze the composer, the style of the particular era, the character of any given phrase in the music, the four instrumental voices, or melody, rhythm, and harmony. However, when we compose, interpret, or listen, these individual elements must be united into a totality, a "whole sound" in movement. The same is true of conversation, and conversational artists must play with everything connected to the time-form of conversation: place, time, circumstances, participants, conversational goal, level of the material, flow, tension, and direction. This only works if we surrender ourselves entirely to what is happening, while at the same time conceiving impulses out of what we perceive—impulses that we then introduce into the conversation at just the right time. In other words: *We must alternate between active devotion and creative initiative.*

Obviously, this requires much practice, and, in this way, conversation does not differ from other arts. I am concerned here only with developing the possibility of this kind of conversational form, a form that might seem almost utopian. However, once we simply recognize that conversation can be an art and therefore requires many stages of practice, we have already achieved a great deal. The unique thing about this art is that there is no outside audience—this art form is realized only in the interaction between people. Having realized this, we can consider conversation as a preparation, or school, for a social art, the art of society. Therefore, let us again consider the participants and their relationships.

Conversational Exercises

Exercises with designated concepts—
fruit, flower, point, time, evolution, and so on.

- Each person says the first thing that comes to mind.

- Each person says a characterizing sentence. These are sentences that express some aspect of the concept. "Fruit always reminds me of my last vacation in Brazil" is not a characterization of fruit, whereas, "A fruit bears a seed within itself" is such a characterization.

- It is interesting to differentiate between general, conceptual characteristics pertaining to all fruits, and a descriptive process that culminates in a concrete mental image of a specific fruit at a specific time of year in a specific landscape. This is a variation of the preceding exercise, with the added condition that participants relate their contributions to the previous ones.

- We can also begin by describing a particular fruit—or other object or process—with the goal of continuing the conversation by envisioning the essential characteristics also as images of human soul qualities.

- We can also work with related pairs of concepts: Sun—Moon, large—small, and so on.

- Question and answer: The first person asks a question about the concept, which must then be answered by the second person before asking a new question.

CHAPTER 6

Conversation as a Basic Form of Modern Community-Building

The Effect of Individual Contributions

In the last chapter we considered how the value of a contribution was determined by its position in a conversation. We also looked at the idea of "ripeness in time." But there is another reason why contributions that have the same content are sometimes heard and sometimes not. Whether a contribution is heard or not often depends on who makes the contribution. There simply may be antipathy toward the speaker, or perhaps he or she is just not taken seriously. Of course, this is the most basic level, but it is a level we often experience, and one to which we must always bring awareness. However, when different speakers make contributions, the varying impact achieved may also be due to hidden or obvious power structures. and should also be clearly seen. This is a second-level phenomenon.

There is yet another reason why one contribution achieves a better effect than another: Varying degrees of competence are found in individual speakers. A healthy discussion group develops a feeling for each individual's abilities, and depending on the subject under consideration, weighs each contribution accordingly. Thus we can experience how participants instinctively turn to one person or another, depending on the question raised; and, ideally, this creates a functioning hierarchy of abilities. When dealing with individual abilities, the principle of equality should never come into play, because judgments and evaluations depend on individual competence. Estimation of one's own abilities and recognition of others' abilities comprise the social preconditions for every community and, therefore, every conversation. This has nothing to do with evaluating the intrinsic worth of individual participants, but with the fact that a common goal is best achieved when participants' abilities are optimally developed. Only when we enter the stage of actual decision-making—where everyone is equally involved—only there do we find the position of each individual relevant and equal in weight. For this reason, it is a good idea to go around the circle and get everyone's opinion before making decisions that go beyond the questions of the day.

There is still another possible reason why one conversational contribution is heard better than another. It was pointed out earlier that the voice and linguistic formulation—the *how*—is at least as effective as the *what.* This effect is achieved through the power, or lack of power, of the spoken word. Anyone possessing the power of the word, the power of speech, has both great conversational possibilities and great responsibilities. We all know the situation we find in many conversational groups: *The same people do all the talking.* Often, this is due to the fact some individuals express themselves better and more easily than others and, therefore, always appear superior. Others are so shy that they do not dare speak. Those who are verbally powerful show social responsibility by noticing that they are dominating, and by deciding to forego the use of their power. They also show responsibility when they employ their power to formulate the concerns of those unable to express themselves well. This means making the concerns of others one's own, then formulating what the other intends, and putting it into the best possible light. Instead of using rhetoric to uncover a partner's weaker contradictions and one-sidedness, or opposing them directly, the attempt can be made to hear what they are trying to say through imperfections: "If I have understood you correctly, then you mean. . . ." Whether or not one agrees does not matter; it matters only that they are perceived properly in the group.

If the group exceeds a certain size, it is natural that some members will say little or nothing at all. Representation, or something very much like it, then occurs—especially in a group of people who have known one another a long time—and a participant can experience his or her thoughts communicated by another. Thus we can hear one person say to another after a conversation is over, "You expressed precisely what I was thinking, but I could never have said it that way!" We should not be pedantic, by insisting that everyone have their say, only to hear again what has already been said over and over again.

Function and Set Roles

Let us return to our fourfold analysis of conversation to discover another fundamental social component. We have seen that the conscious use of time constantly requires various functions to return conversation to a balance of material, flow, tension, and direction. In principle, any participant could exercise any function as soon as the necessity is seen, and this would be the case if all participants had the same ability to lead a conversation. But this rarely happens in real life. More often, abilities become more developed by those who already excel in them. There are those who possess the ability to reduce and balance tensions; others step forward when it is time to make a situation clear; others see to it that sufficient material is presented. If a discussion group is attuned to itself, then the participants can feel who should speak next, given the state of the conversation. As stated before, this is connected to individual abilities. However, there is a step between recognizing functional abilities and actually giving individual participants set roles.

This is where a fundamental problem in social interaction arises. I spoke before of conversational *types*, or *characters*, who even appear to embody specific functions in a conversation and often manifest some characteristic such as one-sidedness. Discussion groups are also always comprised of an idealist, the sceptic, a pedant, the talker, as well as those who are naïve, aggressive, or eternally offended; there are also the preacher, martyr, and, of course, the joker. Each of these plays a role more or less correctly, when appropriate, or springs into action out of turn, becoming particularly unpleasant or laughable. This happens in an orchestra when a drummer or trumpet player starts at the wrong time.

We have seen the importance of delay for the third phase or act in a decision-making process. Any participant consciously following the conversation could recommend a break. It is often a particular person, often someone older, who consistently provides this service.

Let us now consider the concluding phase of a conversation. This is when we can feel, "Now the fruit is ripe!" If the person playing the "delayer" speaks up at this point to suggest a break, or adjournment for the day—to approach the subject again another time—such a suggestion can call forth rejection or even anger from the others. At this stage, we suspect the worst when such people even raise their hand to speak.

We also like to smile at those who remind us that a decision was already made about this issue two years ago. Nevertheless, the function of memory and conscience is indispensable to a group. Someone who pedantically admonishes us about agreed-upon organizational forms, even when it is not appropriate to do so, similarly calls forth opposition. But anyone who has experienced a discussion that has become formless and uncontrolled while trying to arrive at an important decision, longs for an organizer.

If a conversation is to avoid becoming one-sided, it needs all of its various elements. Often, if a certain person, who is usually part of the group, is missing during a conversation, then someone else must step in and assume his or her task to avoid one-sidedness. This works with astonishing regularity. Even a person who is a constant "pain in the neck" during discussions, will be missed. If such people are removed, or remove themselves, then another "pain in the neck" will emerge unnoticed and take over the role, so that the group is complete. This holds true for each role. Thus, we have the picture of a group, either expressing various strengths proceeding from specific, predetermined roles or, ideally, proceeding from immediate perception and presence of mind.

It is a sign of "illness" in the group when roles become set. Set roles result in set, predictable, and unfruitful conversations. Moreover, certain roles or conversational "characters" naturally collide. The realist prefers to answer the idealist's glorious picture of the future by pointing out the financial consequences. The sceptic and the optimist are another pair of opposites who regularly bounce off one another. If the pessimist grumbles at each suggestion that could lead to progress, saying, "It doesn't matter to me, do what you want, but it won't amount to anything," then the optimist in the group will "see red." Conversely, when the optimist paints a picture in which all problems are washed away, the skeptic prepares to attack. When partners in conversation become fixed in such one-sided roles—when roles in conversation become attached to the person—the results can be unfruitful as well as very socially destructive. For this reason, a group that has worked together for a long time cannot avoid consciously processing these problems. Perhaps the courage to change the group dynamic and experiment with new forms will enable the ship that has run aground to float again.

Our questions assume that we are dealing with a community in which everyone is recognized as adults pursuing a common goal—a community that recognizes individual abilities and, yet, also assumes that all share equal rights. When roles become fixed, mutual recognition as equals is threatened. This affects us when we realize we are always associated with certain roles—that is, from the outset of any deliberations, our reaction is counted on in a predictable way. In such cases, we may notice how the attitudes of the others influence our behavior. We may never escape our assigned role and, therefore, may no longer experience pleasure in taking initiative, as we dependably fulfill the fixed expectations of others. Rigid hierarchical structures and predictable mechanisms for decision-making are easily formed in this way. As a consequence, individuals' abilities can no longer flow into the conversation in a living way, to unite and form a common will. Instead, the conversation always leads to the same dead ends—or unfolds routinely in preformed paths while hidden power structures expand and solidify.

The Significance of a Dynamic Image
of the Human Being

Whether such tendencies eventually leave a group—and how this happens—depends primarily on the group's image of the human being and how powerfully this image influences the relationships between participants. The art of conversation described in this book begins with the assumption that there are two opposing principles working in every human being. One represents the past—all that a person has become as a result of one's past, including all that has led to a particular one-sidedness. Education, personal preferences, temperament, age, family background, and profession, all work to determine a person's role in an "antisocial" group, as described at the beginning of this section. On the other hand, there is a higher authority—the bearer of this particular destiny—that can acquire knowledge about itself, and, out of this insight, a process is initiated that leads to self-knowledge.

As Schiller noted in *The Aesthetic Education of Man*, the ideal human being stands in contrast to the actual human being in time. In the tension between these two, life unfolds. Human beings, of their own free accord, can develop themselves along lines acquired not from the world of the senses, but from spiritual insight. Therefore, the person who actually stands before us is always the result of factors working out of the past and possibilities that work from the future. The classic idealists always formulated this by stating that human beings are human when becoming, growing, evolving. The individual power to create residing in every human being is the basis of our humanity. The images of others that we carry, based on past experience, separate us from them. But the image we have of what we can become in the future brings us together; we know that we are fundamentally united with every being that has a human face. We find our true being as an ideal in a higher world. It is here that the *higher self* of others is also to be sought. Working toward a common spiritual center unites and individualizes us at the same time. Worldly centralization, on the other hand, paralyzes and makes us uniform.

Wherever this dynamic principle of individualization reigns, the life of a community is also fostered. We must bear in mind that every person's one-sidedness is really only one side of a developing human being. Therefore we must take into consideration that the picture we have of this person today will no longer be the case tomorrow. Once we cease viewing a one-sided role as fixed and given, and see it as something to develop, then we must consider the reality: the so-called "blatherer," whose inflated words are no longer listened to, will one day come forward with decisive words. Such people are also developing. We should adopt an attitude that does not permanently attach judgment to what has already become, but remains flexible and open to understanding what is becoming. This is the precondition for the practice of human dignity and is also a condition necessary for the art of conversation.

In conversation we can distinguish *function, roles,* and *the individual.* In considering function, we have the entire course of the conversation in mind; if we consider roles, we see how roles played by various individuals are determined by time and destiny; and when we consider the individual, we see possibilities of development that exist for the conversation as well as for the participants. Community today must emerge from the power arising from the wellspring of the individual. The we of a group is not the starting point; it is the result of individuals working together. Every conversation can reflect this process.

Conversational Exercises

Exercises in Conscious Conversation: Art and Nature Observations

- In a free conversational exchange, we describe what we perceive in a work of art or natural object without any attempt to interpret it.

- The first phase leads to descriptions of the relationships between various details. We begin to discover, through works of art, the essentials of their composition by natural objects and the specific manner in which they bring the archetype to expression.

- As we begin to grasp specific relationships more clearly, the inner significance begins to reveal itself. Our conversation continues into this sphere of observation, not just focusing on what can be perceived through the senses.

- This process can be repeated somewhat later out of memory, the goal being to recreate the object observed.

CHAPTER 7

Union in Conversation

We have come to understand conversation as an artistic form in which the participants, practicing presence of mind, seek to balance the various parts of an organism unfolding in time. Conversations by people meeting regularly to make decisions reveal various social interactions that lead us to recognize the fundamental precondition for productive work: *Recognition and respect for our partners as human beings who can develop themselves as creative individuals, no matter what stage they may now be at.* In this chapter we will consider another possible aspect of conversation that can lead us to an even deeper dimension.

Uniting in Individual Conversation

Imagine the following: Someone comes to talk to us about a depressing, unsolved life problem. Of course, it could be just the opposite—we could go to someone to seek advice from them. Let us assume that the problem arises from a deeper level than just ordinary everyday life. Now, imagine that the person seeking advice finds a listener who listens in such a way that he or she gives himself or herself wholly to the other person's problem—without reservation, with no silent attempt to judge, or immediate thoughts about how to respond. This attitude can help the speaker in his or her initial and perhaps awkward presentation of the problem. Perhaps, in order to complete the picture, the listener will then ask a few questions for clarification. Perhaps he or she will reformulate the problem with appropriately sympathetic words. At first, the listener can give no answer, and only let the other person know that their problem has been heard and understood. Then the following can happen. The person who is asked for help says, "Well, I'm really sorry, I'm not sure I can help!" Yet, by means of the conversation itself, the person seeking help may suddenly have an insight about what to do next. He or she then formulates an answer or a direction to work on: "Yes, perhaps that is it!" And movement and energy return.

What happened? Of course, we could say that the formulation of the problem, and the fact that it was understood by someone else, enables the questioner to overcome his or her isolation and become liberated. This newly acquired freedom then allows finding an answer for himself or herself. But there is an even deeper reason connected with the secret of genuine compassion: *Those who seek help open themselves intimately to another because of trust and empathy.* The other person perceives this trust because an inner space is created in the listener for the one seeking help. The listener makes the other's concern his or her own, asking questions that unite with the other's search for insight. This creates a spiritual atmosphere out of which an answer can arise. However, the answer only becomes possible through this higher meeting between two individuals. Both find themselves united in a higher place—*insight,* as we have called it—and for this reason neither can say that one has accomplished more than the other, because total reciprocity has occurred. They can thank one another for the conversation. One finds the other in shared insight. Then there is a feeling that the reciprocal relationship was deepened, even sanctified, because they lived together for a while in a higher dimension.

This feeling of a higher realm is certainly a rare experience—entirely independent of educational achievements or rhetorical power—and received as if by grace. However, the question can be asked: Can such an event, or experience, happen in a larger community of people? This is undoubtedly more difficult, because the intimate atmosphere of dialogue is missing. Much of the dialogue work in groups based on the work of David Bohm seeks this dimension of common insight and experience. When a communion of souls is experienced in common insight, a true experience of community is created.[1]

We can now discern three conditions in the dialogue described. The question, as well as the common search for an answer, lead the human beings to a higher level of being. Both seek the encounter. The first condition is therefore: *Community out of the individual I.* Conversation truly develops only through the *trust* of one person and the selfless *listening* of the other. The second condition is: *Community in light of the other.* And the third condition is: *A higher "uniting" authority or being,* from which the answer arises: *Community in light of a supersensible-divine world.*

There are two literary witnesses that deal with our question most beautifully; both represent high ideals, attainable only in the future. One is Goethe's poetic answer to the events of the French Revolution, his *Conversations of German Immigrants;* the other is Wolfram von Eschenbach's *Parzival.*

---

1. See Athys Floride, *Human Encounters and Karma* (Hudson, NY: Anthroposophic Press, 1990).

Goethe's Idea of a Conversation

Early in his book, Goethe describes the destiny of a German family in flight. They have become friends with a married couple. The husband, an older man, provokes young Karl, the family's son, with his political point of view. Because Karl cannot control his response, the old man, deeply disappointed, breaks with the family. The lady of the household then lists the rules of cultivated society: "Children, let us not forget how many of our own idiosyncracies we have already had to sacrifice to be social in society—long before all these things came to discussion. Let us not forget that everyone, as long as the world exists, will have to learn to rule over themselves, at least outwardly, in order to be sociable." This is the law of civilized conversation, one could say— of controlled, spontaneous conversation in which one leaves the stage of pure association and seeks civilized encounter in conversation.

Conversations with German Immigrants continues with the decision to pass the time by telling stories. The seven stories, then told and discussed, represent an ascending series of steps toward purification. It is a development based on voluntary resignation and sacrifice for the sake of a higher reality. The motto of these stories could be: "Through the senses to the spirit." They begin with a palpable ghost story, in which a disappointed lover seeks revenge after his death by making himself constantly visible to his love in the form of a ghost. Another ghost story and two thrilling adventures follow. The fifth story tells of the gradual overcoming of a burning passion by voluntary renunciation that returns dignity to the main character. We find the same theme in the sixth story: Ferdinand, the main character, suffers from unrestrained paternal

authority. An accident causes him to become a thief, but
he regrets his deed and secretly returns the stolen money
to his father and finds his way to a respectable life. The
result of his painful experiences is an original pedagogical principle. He teaches his children voluntary resignation; every evening, one or another of his children must
decline dessert. He proceeds in the same way with regard
to the use of time. The children are left entirely free.
One day, however, he calls them all together and checks
their watches: from now on, everything must be done exactly to the minute. In his pedagogy there is never an ab-
solutely authoritarian principle at work; rather the father
strives for an education out of freedom, for the sake of
self-mastery.

The seventh story, "The Fairy Tale of the Green Snake
and the Beautiful Lily," may be characterized as the last
and highest step on the path of development from the
lower to the higher human being. The scene of the story
is laid in a countryside divided by a river. On one side
lives a maiden known as "the beautiful Lily," the object
of all men's desires, whose beauty is deadly. All who
touch her fall lifeless at her feet. Two Will o' the Wisps
and a Youth come in search of the Lily. They are helped
in their quest by the Green Snake who lives on the other
side of the river and by an Old Man with a lamp of
miraculous powers. In the end, the Youth will find the
Lily in her garden and, forgetting her deadly touch, run
to embrace her and fall lifeless at her feet. Before that,
however, in a subplot, we find the Snake going about his
business on the other side of the river, where he has the
habit of visiting a mysterious underground Temple
whose mystery, it is said, may be understood only by
means of a magic potion of gold. Now, when the Will o'
the Wisps first arrive, gold falls from their wings, and the

Snake, hoping it is the right kind, swallows some and rushes back to the Temple. There, revealed in the light now radiating from his body, he sees four metal kings and is initiated into great secrets. Shortly afterward, the Old Man appears, announcing "The time has come." He reveals that, since the Snake has learned the secret of the Temple, the river, which was crossable only by a ferry or by the shadow of a giant or across the back of the Snake himself, would now be joined by a bridge—and the Temple, to fulfill an ancient prophecy, would no longer lie underground but by the river's bank. The Snake, thus initiated, now joins the Youth in search of the Lily. He is present when the Youth falls lifeless at her feet, standing there at a loss until the Old Man appears, declaring that the Youth will be restored only by being taken to the Temple. The Snake forms a protective circle around the Youth and, at dawn, they all return to the river, where the Snake arches his back to form a bridge. Having done so, he feels his job is done and resolves to sacrifice himself for the Youth's sake. His skin is transformed into a ring of precious stones and cast into the river. This, the Old Man declares, will make the everlasting bridge a reality. At the same time, the Youth begins to return to life and all descend into the Temple. Suddenly, then, the earth seems to shake, the Temple rocks, passes beneath the stream, rises, and appears upon the bank. The Youth and the Lily, united, are now called King and Queen. There is great rejoicing. The bridge appears and a throng of people pass gaily over it. "All honor to the Snake," the Old Man cries.

Everything in the Fairy Tale is expressed in artistic pictures. Again, we are concerned with the union of the world of the senses and the world of the spirit, which is made possible only by the Snake's sacrifice. The Snake forms itself into a bridge over the river so that men and women can visit the Temple, which has come to light out of subterranean concealment on the other shore. In the subterranean Temple are heard the famous words—so often quoted out of context—concerning conversation: "What is more glorious than gold?" the King asks. "Light," answers the Snake. "What is livelier than light?" the King then asks in response. "Conversation," answers the Snake. We should note the sequence: *Gold, Light, Conversation.* From previous images in the story, we become acquainted with "Will-o'-the-Wisps" who are unable to keep gold within themselves, and must constantly shake it out of themselves, thereby creating problems for those around them. The Snake, on the other hand, licking the gold from the hidden veins, begins to shine. It transforms gold into light by digesting it—a picture for the complete recasting of sense-knowledge into spiritual insight. What is more lively than the light of insight? Conversation is enlivening, refreshing, and renewing—not conversation that arises from the chaotic warmth of spontaneous talk, and not conversation that is ruled by intellectual understanding, but only conversation that unites the light of insight with the warmth of human encounter. This requires voluntary sacrifice and devotion to a common ideal.

Preconditions of Modern Community-Building

In Goethe's work we again find the three preconditions of modern community-building:

1. An I that can overcome its time-form
2. A relationship to the supersensible-divine world
3. Selfless sacrifice for others

Based on these three steps we can imagine a conversation among a number of people who are able to approach a question out of a common higher goal. For our conversation, let's imagine the following ideal sequence. First, the question is illuminated on all sides and experienced by all the participants in an equally lively fashion. Then various points of view are developed. The danger that individuals might identify with their own points of view has been removed by the seriousness of the question and because participants are willing to listen to others' views as if they were their own. Individual viewpoints are united with the common problem under investigation.

At this point, by means of any one of the different contributions that have been made, a mood or feeling enters the group that *something entirely new has arisen.* One after another, different contributions are made, connected with the new idea, and deepened and expanded. This new atmosphere now intensifies, and what happens next can be expressed by saying that none of the participants individually could ever have come upon the new idea on their own. It is as if a new insight becomes possible through the efforts of the group and in no way merely represents the sum of individual efforts. It seems like a transformation—a recasting, brought about by something *higher.* We feel as if we were touched by something spiritual and were united with it momentarily. Retrospectively, the participants experienced not only the joy of solving a problem, but also a sense of community with others, a magical moment of oneness, of grace.

Such conversations are rare, but anyone who has ever experienced it—even once—knows that it is *enlivening,* and that it has a profoundly religious dimension. It is religion in practice—for we actually reunite ourselves with each other and with the divine.

Conversation as an Experience of Communion

If we look more closely at the course of individual as well as group conversations, we see that they correspond to the sequence found in the sacrament of the Christian mass: 1) Gospel reading, 2) Offering, 3) Transubstantiation, and 4) Communion.

The first part of the Mass contains the reading of the Gospel. God's Word is revealed and shared with the congregation. This corresponds to the first phase of a conversation in which everyone unites with a question or set of questions, and the participants agree to the basic criteria for making decisions—warmth is kindled, direction is set, and the light of common understanding is shared.

The second part of the Mass is the Offering. The smoke from burning incense rises as an image of the prayers and sacrifice of the congregation rising to the spiritual world. This sacrificial element of warmth follows the Gospel reading's element of light, and expresses the devotion of the earthly to the divine. In conversation, this stage is represented by the sacrifice of letting go of one's own preconceived viewpoint, by the conscious effort to open oneself in devoted listening to the words of others. It also means overcoming everyday associations and prejudices, and holding the common higher goal before one's eyes.

In the third part of the Mass, the Transubstantiation takes place: bread and wine are transformed into the body and blood of Christ. Spirit permeates physical matter. In conversation, as positions change, the question is permeated by something higher through the selfless efforts of the participants who keep the conversation moving and the question alive in ever new ways.

Finally, Communion: the faithful are united with

Christ in bread and wine, through the matter that has been transformed. In conversation, the participants are united by the gift of insight, or the presence of spirit commonly perceived. The first two parts of the Mass require the dedication of the faithful to God. In the second half, divine grace is at work from above. It is like an answer to a question. The same is true of conversation. Through spiritual activity in the first half, participants create the vessel into which something new and higher can flow.

We also find this archetypical sequence in an individual's search for knowledge. In this search, we first of all unite ourselves existentially with a question. We suppress all associations and preconceived thought patterns that want to fill our consciousness; we renounce all that wants to rise out of our bodies. This intensified activity then creates a space within us that can receive knowledge and insight from the hands of a higher being. To achieve this, we must direct all our inner activity toward a spiritual receptivity—create, as it were, an active passivity within us, so that we can then unite ourselves with something higher. In a more intensified form, this path is also that of individual meditation.

When such a fourfold path is not provided for by an established "ritual" form, we may notice that a void, or zero point, is experienced between the first and the second halves of the conversation. This is the moment of crisis, or of a dramatic climax, in which we see whether transformation is really possible. At this point, we undergo an experience of absolute powerlessness, leading either to a dead-end, or to an experience of resurrection into a new dimension. In drama, this is the place for an intermission, after the third act.

The comparison of conversation with the events of the

Mass makes it clear that only truly significant material for discussion—corresponding to the Gospel reading—can provide the necessary foundation for the event described. In meditation, it is the mantram or the whole content of the meditation. In conversation, it is the question that relates to something higher that goes beyond the individual's everyday routine or usual pattern of interest.

Such a conversation can give us a unique, irreplaceable experience. The activity of the participants calls an event into being that works in the deepest sense to create community. For this reason, in any community, it is worth cultivating and holding such an ideal in mind.

Parzival—The Question of Redemption

In Wolfram von Eschenbach's epic, *Parzival*, the hero saves his uncle, Amfortas, from suffering brought about by the uncle's own actions, and, in doing so, succeeds him as Grail King. We have seen that questions are of the greatest significance for conversation, fostering and guiding it by provoking answers. If we again take up the sequence of the various kinds of questions possible, we find ourselves recapitulating the stages of conversation, and thus we can discover the significance of Parzival's question to Amfortas, *What ails thee?*

Without a question, a conversation cannot come about. In the realm of spontaneous feelings, we have already met what we might call the contact-question. Travelers may ask the person sitting next to them if he or she is getting out at the next station. The waiter asks a guest if the food tasted good. In these questions we see a transition to mere convention, because the question anticipates a positive response, and rhetorical questions

almost force us to respond this way. Curiosity, also
prompted by feeling, tries to draw something out of the
conversational partner that he or she may not want to
say. Gossipy questions belong in this category. "Is it really true that Mrs. Miller has left her husband and run
off with another man?" We would like to know something that will satisfy a craving for sensational gossip.
Questions of concern also belong to this category. They
are asked to show the other person that we are interested in how they are doing: "Did you have a good vacation?" And, finally, there is the question asked merely to
keep the conversation alive, to end a break in the conversation. All of these questions are found primarily in
spontaneous conversation. The motivation here origi-
nates in the realm of everyday feelings, even though our
minds are involved.

Questions of knowledge constitute a second group.
The question: "Where's the path to the beach?" seeks
information. It is asked for the objective reason that the
questioner wants to go to the beach. Questions of this
kind can be elevated to an academic level, to become a
question of textbook fact: "How high is Mt. Everest?"
"What is the quadratic formula?" Questions like this
can be asked because of interest in the subject, or in order to achieve a pedagogical aim. The common element in all knowledge questions is that they count on
straightforward answers that will bring closure to the
conversation. Many questions of this sort do not foster
conversation in the true sense, but simply demand un-
ambiguous answers. We must distinguish these from
another kind of question—a need for knowledge that
cannot be satisfied by a single answer, but seeks to stimulate a community thought process. "What is the
present state of race relations?" "Is there life after

death?" These are life questions asked from a deeper region of the human being than mere questions of fact.

Such questions may be posed as a result of general interest or wholly out of personal perplexity. If the latter is the case, they can become questions of destiny. True questions of knowledge lead to the most fruitful conversations only when they follow the precondition laid down by St. Augustine in his *Confessions*: "None of us should say that we have found the truth. Let us rather seek it as if it were unknown to both of us. If none of us presumes to have found the truth, we will be able to seek it in good conscience and in harmony."[2] What is important is the attitude toward the question held by everyone in the group. While questions of simple fact and knowledge aim toward an exchange of knowledge— that is, address the intellect—deeper questions require insight going beyond mere intellect, challenging our whole being. Such questions may be said to originate in the higher self, and appeal to the higher self of the other.

Just as questions concerned with a grappling for genuine knowledge represent a higher level than questions seeking factual information, so does genuine interest in other people lead to deeper "feeling" questions. We can ask someone the question: "How are you doing?" and it could mean many different things. It could take the abbreviated form "How-dya-do?" spoken as a greeting requiring no response. Or the question could be asked because the questioner sees that something is not right with the other person. Under the appropriate circumstances, and asked out of selfless interest in the

---

2. Cf. St. Augustine, *Confessions,* ed., trans., Henry Chadwick (Oxford University Press, 1992).

other person, this question could then dissolve a knot in a relationship and begin a healing process. The person who is questioned finds his or her tongue loosened, so that a conversation can begin concerning the problem. Questions arising from selfless perception of another's condition can have a redeeming effect. But if such questions are asked merely out of convention, they cannot have a real helping effect. Just as the true knowledge question leads beyond simple requests for fact, into a realm that touches personal existence, so too a question asked from immediate perception of another's condition, can lift us beyond what is merely subjective and personal. Both questions—the true knowledge question and the feeling question—originate in the deeper parts of the soul where I-consciousness resides, and both types of questions serve to unite us with others. The two kinds of question are also brought together, for example, when a conference of professional therapists discuss a patient, or when a college of teachers discuss a pupil. The search for insight then comes from the will to help another.

These examples demonstrate the importance of setting a *tone* at the beginning of a conversation, and indicates the kind of consciousness required for a higher level of dialogue. It is possible to hold a pupil or patient conference with the everyday consciousness governed by free association—"You know, his father has an auto repair shop! Perhaps he will give us a discount if we keep the child." Or a routine question might be asked concerning organization, leading to simple prescriptions right at the start of the discussion. "This is a typical case. How can we convince his parents that he belongs in a school for special children?" "A case like this can only be handled through social services. I can give you the number," and so on. We can only ask deeper questions after we have overcome the pedestrian mood of daily life, and the deep-seated desire to apply simple categories has been set aside. Only then can we hope for our conversation to become a truly spiritual event in which something entirely new can arise.

Parzival's question is the archetype of all questions seeking insight into human destiny and salvation. Parzival, as the model knight, frees Queen Condwiramur and marries her. Stories of knighthood and chivalry usually end with this; for Parzival, this decisive action is only the beginning. He feels the need to see his mother, whom he left long ago, but the reader knows that his mother collapsed and died from the pain caused by his departure. The call of his heart, seeking his mother, thus comes to him from the supersensible world of the dead. The call leads him to his first visit to the Grail castle. He sees all the wonders of the castle, and notices with sympathy the pain of the wounded Amfortas. Yet, Parzival consciously does not ask questions about Amfortas' suffering, because Gurnemanz, who taught him to be a knight, told him not to ask unnecessary questions. It was precisely this omission that proves to be Parzival's undoing. Before the assembled knights, Kundry, who is the messenger of the Grail, scorns him because he failed to ask the question that would have redeemed Amfortas from his suffering. Parzival withdraws from all of them, and from his vow to serve God, but continues his search for the Grail castle—though he was told he would never find it a second time. After many battles fought on his lonely journeys, he finally manages, through the grace of God, to find the castle again. He then asks the question, saves Amfortas, and becomes the King of the Grail.

What happened between the first and the second visits? Why was he condemned for something done in accordance with the knightly code of behavior? It is the need to take a step beyond the action guided by the authority of a prescribed code, toward action for which the I itself is responsible. This sense of responsibility—the inner authority of the I—can only develop and mature in loneliness and isolation, both from his former knightly companions and from the God who allowed his terrible mistake in the first place. The impulse to seek the Grail is the drive toward community in the supersensible realm. Parzival continues his search, against all human reason; and, in the end, he is able to ask the redemptive question out of compassion, acquired by an I purified through loneliness—an I that has left behind all blood-ties, everything given by the structures of society, and even the God that had been given him.

Here, again, we find the elements of modern community-building, as they can be realized in an exemplary way:

1. The community of the Grail is a community in the sign of the Holy Spirit and, as such, is related to the divine supersensible world.

2. Parzival finds the motivation to ask his question in the other person when he experiences the other's pain as his own.

3. Parzival asks the question out of his higher I, which has freed itself from entanglements arising from blood-ties and from the dictates of society.

Conversational Exercises

Conversations with Allocated Roles or Functions

These are variations on exercises in dramatic improvisation that serve to heighten our awareness of the importance of the various functions in a conversation. As preparation for these exercises, I recommend retrospective analysis of various conversations in regard to the various functions. Was there enough content? How was the tempo? Did it race off helter-skelter or merely limp along? Were there moments of dramatic tension or an atmosphere of peaceful harmony? Did the conversation have direction or meander hither and thither? What contributions served which functions? It is good to differentiate between the effects of individuals' emotional engagement on conversational dynamics, and the flow of the conversation itself, even though both are integral parts of a conversation.

- The eight functions—you may discover more— can be written on small pieces of paper and drawn from a hat. Thus, each participant has a function unknown to the others. Depending on the size of the circle, one or two participants can be designated as observers. In the conversation that follows, each tries to contribute in a way appropriate to his function. It is good to designate a theme for the conversation: provocative statements (*"Only native speakers should teach a language."*); pearls of wisdom (*"All learning is in reality a process of remembering," from Plato*); or, for groups of people who share a common task, such as a school faculty, the theme might be situations taken from daily life.

- Each participant speaks only when he feels his function is asked for. In larger circles there will be more than one for each function.

- Each participates freely in the conversation but pays special attention to the function with which she or he has been entrusted.

- Differentiate between conversations with and without a designated moderator.

- Differentiate between cognitive conversations and those for decision-making.

The retrospective analysis is especially important for these exercises. Those designated as observers should have certain criteria in mind as they follow the course of the conversation. The goal is to slowly overcome vague feelings of satisfaction or dissatisfaction that we have in the aftermath of speaking with one another, and become conscious of what each can do to enhance the productivity of such encounters. Through retrospect we can gain objective understanding of what took place and why.

Most of us have, at some point or other, had a chance to discover obstacles lying in the path of self-education. Generally, we see that it is relatively difficult to continue, and we either forget that we actually decided to do a certain exercise for a given period of time, or we discover that we have developed a certain antipathy for the exercise. It is easy to imagine that these obstacles along our path of inner development also arise when we begin to practice with other people. If we remember how much effort it took to overcome these hindrances, we then have a sense of what is required when a circle of people decide to practice together. One possibility for overcoming any arising inertia is to approach the exercises in much the same way as a connoisseur approaches a fine meal, or as a music lover listens to a good symphony.

These exercises have been worked with in different rhythms—weekly, monthly, and so on. A bi-monthly rhythm of intensive five- to six-hour meetings has proven to be quite productive, as long as work is done by individuals between meetings. Of course, each group will need to find its own rhythm.

CHAPTER 8

Paths of Development

To conclude our observations we must consider the steps we can take to improve our ability to converse with others. Artists must constantly improve their ability to shape and form their materials. Yet, in the act of creating, they must forget the steps they perfected in practice. The following exercises are intended to be used in the same way. As long as we have to think about them, we are not yet artists in conversation. We have seen that the special aspect of the art of conversation is the uniting of different people for a common action or goal. Therefore, we must distinguish between exercises individuals can do for themselves as preparation, and exercises that are only possible in community. Just as conversation lives in the rhythm of I, We, and It, so also there are exercises that the individual can only do outside of the community, and others that are possible only within the community. Furthermore, in the social process of conversation, the moral and artistic realms become one. Thus, the exercises must also bear this characteristic. First, we will turn our attention to individual exercises, after a brief review:

Abilities Required for Conversation

1. In the realm of listening, we need the power of devotion and the ability to open ourselves to others.

2. This applies to the realm of the voice that reveals to us both a speaker's intentions and being, as well as the realm of thought. According to Rudolf Steiner's expanded teaching concerning the senses, we are dealing with the senses of speech, thought, and the I.[1]

3. We also need the ability to observe how time is being used—how the course of conversation is shaped by our use of time.

   • To grasp the NOW, the result of what came BEFORE, and the seed of the will to come AFTER.

   • To develop a sense for constellations of thoughts and people and, generally, for the formation of constellations in conversation. All of these abilities fall within the realm of devotion to the "You" (conversation partner) and the "It" (thought content).

4. Finally, we are concerned with training abilities that originate in the realm of the I.

   • Our own ability to think and judge, out of which our contributions arise.

   • Our own ability to speak—that is, the ability to modify our speech so that it is appropriate to the particular group of which we are a part.

---

1. Rudolf Steiner has named and described twelve (sometimes ten) senses in the human being. They are: the senses of touch, life, self-movement, balance, smell, taste, sight, temperature, hearing, speech, concept, and I (or ego). A thorough study on this subject can be found in Rudolf Steiner's *Anthroposophy (A Fragment)*, (Hudson, NY: Anthroposophic Press, 996); and Albert Soesman's *The Twelve Senses*, (Stroud, UK: Hawthorn Press, 1993).

A specific form of training these capacities can be found in the exercises suggested by Rudolf Steiner as preparation on the path to higher knowledge and developed by him in many writings and lectures.[2] An essential element of this path of training is the union of intellectual, artistic, and moral development. For this reason, we find in Steiner a wealth of concrete suggestions for our purposes.

Practicing Listening

Among the exercises for a healthy soul and for practical ability in life we find the practice of uniting oneself with the audible world—from noises, to tones, to animal sounds expressive of soul, to the quality of human speech:

> Particularly important as we develop . . . is that we also work on the way we listen to other people when they speak. On the path to higher knowledge this listening skill is extremely important. We must become accustomed to listening in such a way that we quiet our own inner life completely when we listen. For example, when someone expresses an opinion and another listens, agreement or disagreement usually stirs immediately within the listener. Often in such a situation we feel compelled to express our own opinion at once, especially if we

2. Rudolf Steiner. *How to Know Higher Worlds: A Modern Path of Initiation* (Hudson, NY: Anthroposophic Press, 1994) ; *An Outline of Occult Science* (Hudson, NY: Anthroposophic Press, 1972); *Theosophy: An Introduction to the Spiritual Processes in Human Life and in the Cosmos* (Hudson, NY: Anthroposophic Press, 1994), Chapter Four, "The Path to Knowledge").

disagree. However, on the path to higher knowledge we must learn to silence any agreement or disagreement with the opinions we hear. Naturally, this does not mean that we should suddenly change our way of life and strive to achieve this complete inner silence all the time. We must start with isolated instances that we choose intentionally. Then quite slowly and gradually, as if by itself, this new way of listening will become a habit.

In spiritual research, we practice this new way of listening in a systematic way. As students, we should feel it our duty to set aside, as an exercise, certain times when we listen to the most contrary opinions, completely silencing within us all agreement and, especially, all negative judgments. Not only must we silence our intellectual judgment, but also any feelings of disapproval, rejection, or even agreement. Above all, we must observe ourselves carefully to ensure that such feelings, even though absent from the surface of the soul, are not present in its innermost depths. For example, we must learn to listen to the remarks of those who are in some way inferior to us, suppressing *every* feeling of superiority or knowing better.

Listening to children in this way is especially useful, and even the wisest of us can learn a great deal from them. These exercises teach us to listen selflessly to the words of others, completely excluding our own personality, opinions, and feelings. Once we are practiced at listening in this way without criticism, then gradually, even when the most contradictory views and illogical statements are aired before us, we begin to learn how to unite ourselves with the being of the other person and fully enter into it. We begin to hear through the words, into the other person's soul. As we consistently practice this new habit, sound becomes the medium through which we can perceive soul and spirit.[3]

The point is to selectively practice this way of behaving so that what has been consciously repeated gradually becomes an ability that can be taken for granted.

The Conscious Decision to Forego Speaking

A practical way to begin this exercise is to intentionally forego speaking out, to resign oneself to not speaking—precisely at those moments when one would like to. With any given theme that we care about deeply, we plan to hold back, at the last minute, whatever is just on the tip of our tongue wanting to be said. If we do this often enough, we will become able to perceive the insight that seeks expression in our spoken words early enough to catch it before speech. In doing so, we gain the ability to observe some of the most mysterious processes in conversation. No sooner have we overcome ourselves and held back our contribution, than another person formulates what we wanted to say. This may irritate us to begin with but later we can come to feel satisfaction that our own opinion has been confirmed by another. We can even make a game of trying to guess who in the group might be the one to bring forth our own suppressed contribution. Thus, we may also discover that ideas belonging to a conversation seek expression quite independently of any particular person.

---

3. *How to Know Higher Worlds*, pp. 46–47.

With continued practice we can observe yet another kind of success. This time we speak up only when we feel it serves the matter in hand. We will find that precisely this method lends greater weight and impact to our own individual contributions. Those who quickly and frequently speak up squander themselves, both inwardly in their substance, and outwardly in the attention and respect their contributions encounter. Speech that has been consciously restrained increases in its power by virtue of silence. Of course, this is true only for those who would like to speak, not for those who have no intention of speaking in the first place. Perhaps, for these people the best exercise is to take up the task of expressing themselves as often as possible so as to dismantle their inner or outer thresholds.

Training in the Perception of Voices

Another exercise consists in observing the effects of other contributions on our own breathing—in perceiving individual voices. This means strengthening the musical side of speech, as opposed to the content. When looking back, it is astonishing how difficult it is to recall individual voices into one's memory. Anyone attempting this will listen better in the next conversation. Such exercises also have the consequence that, the activity naturally flowing into one's own thought and sentence formation is gradually carried over to the perception of others. It will be possible to dispense with the raising of hands and the use of lists specifying the next speaker, only when this perception has become obvious to everyone. An inner compulsion to speak makes us deaf to others until we have gotten rid of it, or consciously let go of it by turning our attention outward. Until this is done, we remain essentially excluded from conversation and run the risk of saying something out of place and time. We may even run the risk of egoistically saying something already said by someone else. We would be like chamber musicians who know only their own voice, and present it enthusiastically without taking any notice of the other players.

Training in the Perception of Expressed Thoughts

Systematic training in listening to music, and the appreciation of dramatic arts, increases our ability to perceive the way time is contoured and used artistically. Both music and drama can help us to experience thoughts as tentative—as forms in a process of development—rather than as finished objects. As we learn to form judgments, we can consciously school ourselves to direct our attention, not to the end-products of thought, but to the process leading to the formation of thoughts. This means that understanding presupposes perception of the complex web of relationships, within which the conversation is embedded. A concept is not firmly tied, at any time, to the word that expresses it—concept and word live in a fluid medium. Therefore, within a given constellation or context, words only have validity as tentative characterizations. We can practice working with this truth when we think in a way that is not only analytic and exclusive, but also inclusive and *wholistic.* Here we become aware of the principle of *becoming,* perceptible in all living things; we can analytically define the seed, seedling, leaf, blossom, and fruit of a plant. However, we can also learn to see the future leaf already present in the seed, blossom, leaf, and so on. This requires mobile, fluid thinking. Goethe as a natural scientist provided a

model for such thinking, and Rudolf Steiner's epistemo-
logical works—for example, *Goethe's World View*[4] and *Intuitive Thinking as a Spiritual Path*—are exercise books for
the development of this kind of thinking.

Not until we have a solid foundation under our feet,
can we dare venture out into such dynamic movement.
We create this sure foundation by systematically developing control over our thoughts. This can be done by con-
centrating our whole thinking consciousness for about
five minutes a day on some simple object we have chosen. By overcoming all thought associations and distrac-
tions that would tempt us away from our train of
thought, we strengthen our attention and learn to be
mentally present where we want to be.[5] These exercises
help us to be more fully present in a process with our
whole being—and provide an experience of the power
of devotion.

Exercises for One's Own Ability to Speak

To strengthen our own abilities in speaking we need
an active connection with what we have called *the spirit of
language*. There are various ways to do this. One way is to
occupy ourselves intensely with lyrical poetry that
schools our sense of value for various aspects of speech.
With training and development of artistic speech, such
as Rudolf Steiner's initiatives for speech formation,

---

4. Rudolf Steiner, *Goethe's World View* (Spring Valley, NY: Mercury
Press, 1985).
5. Georg Kühlewind, *Working with Anthroposophy* (Hudson, NY:
Anthroposophic Press, 1992). Jörgen Smit, *How to Transform
Thinking, Feeling and Willing: Practical exercises for the training of
thinking, feeling, willing, imagination, composure, intuition, positivity
and wonder* (Stroud, UK: Hawthorn Press, 1988).

speech can become effective in practice. In this training, we find that listening to speech and speaking—the *you* and the *I* realms—must be perceived and worked with in relation to one another. In my own practice, I learn to listen better, and then develop my own abilities to speak from hearing others speak. The starting point for all individual practice and exercises is honest self-knowledge relating to one's own abilities and limitations. Indeed, the exercises themselves confront us with our limits and idiosyncrasies, and show us ways to go beyond them.

Community Exercises: Review

What exercise can we do together in community? To answer this we must first explore a fundamental principle: Truly productive work occurs only when the individuals involved are prepared. A consensus must exist among the participants that everyone is following a path of development—this is an indispensable precondition. Exercises in community are doomed to failure if participants have not inwardly said "yes" to such learning and development. Although it may appear obvious, it must nevertheless also be said that every participant must agree to a schooling in community. It often happens that participants in standing committees—colleagues or groups that meet regularly—suggest such exercises, perhaps because of bad conversational experiences in the past. Except in rare instances when this suggestion is accepted by all, either superfluous discussions of fundamental principles arise, or the necessary enthusiasm is lacking. We can require ourselves to be sociable, but we can not demand it of others.

Sometimes, however, something—a *review*, for example—can be introduced despite the opposition of some individuals; actually, something must be introduced, because it at least represents a starting point for further development. After every conversation, participants can briefly reflect on the process they have just gone through. It is best if the person who does this is chosen at the beginning of the meeting—perhaps the chairman or group leader—with others free to supplement his or her account with their own reflections. If at all possible, when looking back at an entire decision-making process, one should look at the individual phases—the problems that arose, what factors were decisive, and so on—*without making any judgments* such as, "So-and-so should never have been allowed to telephone the mayor." Rather, this process should simply characterize what happened. Regular reviews of this kind can create a greater degree of consciousness, leading to a renewal of the group.

Just as an individual can only attain a modicum of self-knowledge, and begin the work of inner development by observing one's own accomplishments without emotion, so also, the impulses for improvement in a group can arise only if the group's work is observed soberly and impartially. And just as we can feel inner resistance rising up within ourselves when we seek honest self-knowledge, objections will also arise in a group, seeking to hinder a review of its conversations. Any community unwilling to consciously begin a schooling in conversation will have to make do with organizational supports, which become indispensable in such cases. The group will then operate only from the organizing intellect, not within the realm of artistic endeavor. Nevertheless, it is better for a group to have clear forms and transparent structures for decision-making, than to work under the illusion that it is free and artistic, when, actually, group members are simply engaged in egocentric improvisation. This usually means that accidents of time and place, fatigue, external coercion, the powerful individual, or perhaps a non-committal nod from someone, is allowed to make the final decision. Even then, of course, it still remains open for participants to improve their abilities with their own individual review of the group conversation. Of course, an individual review must make phenomenological observation the primary goal, rather than criticism. If criticism creeps into the review, one can all too easily become the typical figure who, leaning back and assuming the persona of an enlightened being, explains to the others exactly what is right, and that this particular discussion group is a hopeless case.

As a group looks back over the course of a conversation and conducts a review of what occurred, certain kinds of questions can be useful: How did the thoughts develop? Who spoke when? Can different phases of the conversation be distinguished? How was the conversation developed in its substance, pace, tension, and direction? What happened to the relationship *I-You-It?*

Recognizing that our primary goal is to search for the right decision, it should be clear that we must never misuse a conversation as a mere occasion for practicing techniques and conducting experiments. This would undermine the seriousness of the situation. We would be like artists who confuse a rehearsal with an actual performance, where the fruits of many rehearsals should be visible. But, just as we can see where there is room for improvement after a performance, so a group review of conversation can lead to exercises during future conversations, carried out quietly, so that the main purpose of the meeting is not disturbed. However, such exercises must remain voluntary.

Self-Knowledge of the Roles We Play

Role-playing can sometimes help a group gain self-knowledge. Participants are asked to assume a role and address a theme under pressure of having to make a decision. They may be asked to portray various one-sided characters, or assume certain functions in the conversation. For example, they may apply the "brakes" or accelerate the pace. This can be done to the point of humorous caricature. It is very effective if one switches roles or functions in the midst of conversation, so that individuals now represent the polar opposite of what they represented in the first half. Such role-playing conversations make the fabric of relationships conscious in a group, as well as to bring awareness of the tendency to stagnate into hardened positions. Of course, we must be able to laugh at our own one-sidedness and carefully avoid inwardly pointing at others. Role-playing usually mirrors our inadequacies so clearly that it is then unnecessary to discuss them analytically.

Seeking Insight through Conversation

Undoubtedly, the most effective group exercise is to consciously train ourselves in conversation that has the purpose of acquiring insight. In such exercises, consciousness is first directed entirely toward the theme under consideration—a theme that naturally limits concentration to a particular subject is best. For example, a group could talk about a picture on the wall in such a way that they refrain completely from any judgmental observations. It is important to set aside a period of time for this purpose—perhaps half an hour—and strictly adhere to the set time-limit. One can also discuss specific concepts such as "time," "development," "faith," and so on; or pithy formulations of truth as found in epigrams and paradoxical sayings. Having done this, the group might notice a great difference between the discussion and observation of a painting, and the kind of movement found in a discussion of concepts.

From such exercises, we can learn to recognize conversational "bottlenecks"—for example, when the conversation degenerates into an exclusive dialogue; when there is a shortage of material due to a shortage of insights; when contributions are loose and disconnected from one another—especially when observing paintings; when digressions occur repeatedly; and so on. On the basis of their experience, participants can then decide what the conditions should be for the next exercise. For example, each participant could be limited to one contribution; further contributions from an individual could be allowed only after everyone has had a chance to speak; a set sequence for the contributions could be established; a requirement could be established that contributions just spoken be repeated in some way; or the next conversation could be introduced and actively led as needed by one of the participants. After everyone has spoken, the entire conversation can be reconstructed backwards beginning with the last contribution. The group could then begin to work on a mutually agreed-upon text.

As awareness of conversational methodology expands from the content of conversation to the question of how conversation is actually conducted, a group will approach the point when it can do without the guidance of a leader, because it is becoming more homogeneous. A group will discover that as it meets more often in this way, more will be gained toward knowledge and insight, and this becomes the very community-building factor needed for decision-making conversations. A new community can arise only when all participants are involved and willing to immerse themselves fully in the knowledge-process; then a community is created and built up anew with every meeting.

These few suggested exercises are only a beginning of what is possible. With a little imagination, many others can be developed, based on ongoing and objective reviews of a group's conversations, and on knowledge of the basic forces and conditions that govern conversations. Implicit in our theme is the fact that it cannot be standardized. Every community, each conversation, must establish its own conditions and processes for development.

The Art of Conversation as a Preparation for the Social Art of the Future

Conversation is a social art, using and shaping time artistically to form human relationships—an art working creatively with the medium of our self-perceptions, and constantly relating these to a higher image of the human being. Artists in the field of social relationships take the individuality of others into account, because they know that they are united with others in a higher, spiritual world. Everyone has a higher power within themselves, and looking toward this higher power, we unite in and with something higher than ourselves. Christ said, "When two or three are gathered in my name, there I am also." Leonardo da Vinci's painting *The Last Supper* depicts this ideal. The twelve disciples show us twelve different ways of being human according to character, temperament, origin, education, and so on. Leonardo shows us these people in their one-sidedness—impetuous Peter, overly enthusiastic Philip, didactic Thomas, fearful Andrew, and so on. Their expressive gestures proclaim their personal reactions to Christ's words, "*One of you will betray me!*" Yet all of their gestures relate directly to the central figure of Christ. Immediately following this moment, the disciples share in the bread and the wine—the body and blood of Christ—which leads them to a higher community, transforming their old, divisive natures through a power leading them into the future.

The "Last Supper" is not a one-time event in the past, but an ongoing reality. It is the archetype, not only of the highest form of conversation, but of humanity as an evolving community.

Further Reading

Bryant, William, *The Veiled Pulse of Time: An Introduction to Biographical Cycles and Destiny,* Lindisfarne Books, Hudson, NY, 1996.

Finser, Torin M., *In Search of Ethical Leadership: If not now, when?* SteinerBooks, Great Barrington, MA, 2003.

————, *School Renewal: A Spiritual Journey for Change,* SteinerBooks, Great Barrington, MA, 2001.

Floride, Athys. *Human Encounters and Karma.* Anthroposophic Press, Hudson, NY,1990.

Glasl, Friedrich, *Confronting Conflict: A First-Aid Kit for Handling Conflict,* Hawthorn Press, Stroud, UK, 1999.

Greenleaf, Robert. *The Servant as Leader.* Robert Greenleaf Center, Indianapolis, 1991.

Kühlewind, Georg. *From Normal to Healthy: Paths to the Liberation of Consciousness.* Lindisfarne Press, Hudson, NY, 1988.

————, *Meditation and the Soft Will,* Lindisfarne Books, Great Barrington, MA, 2005.

Peace Direct, *Unarmed Heroes: Personal Testimonies and Essays on the Peaceful Resolution of Conflict,* Clairview Books, 2004.

Rehm, Robert, et al., *Futures that Work: Using Search Conferences to Revitalize Companies, Communities, and Organizations,* Hawthorn Press, Stroud, UK, 2003.

Sardello, Robert, *Facing the World with Soul: The Reimagination of Modern Life,* Lindisfarne Books, Great Barrington, MA, 2004.

————, *Love and the World: A Guide to Conscious Soul Practice,* Lindisfarne Books, Great Barrington, MA, 2001.

Schaefer, Christopher and Tÿno Voors, *Vision in Action: Working with Soul and Spirit in Small Organizations.* Lindisfarne Press, Hudson, NY, 1996.

Spock, Marjory. *Group Moral Artistry II: The Art of Goethean Conversation.* St. George Publications, Spring Valley, NY, 1983.

Steiner, Rudolf, *Esoteric Aspects of the Social Question: The Individual and Society,* Rudolf Steiner Press, London, 2001.

————, *Intuitive Thinking as A Spiritual Path, A Philosophy of Freedom.* Anthroposophic Press, Hudson, NY, 1995.

————, *Social Issues: Meditative Thinking & the Threefold Social Order,* Anthroposophic Press, 1991.

Sussman, Linda. *The Speech of the Grail: A Journey toward Speaking that Heals and Transforms.* Lindisfarne Press, Hudson, NY, 1995.

Van den Brink, Margarete, *More Precious than Light: How Dialogue can Transform Relationships and Build Community,* Hawthorn Press, 1996.

————, *Transforming People and Organizations: The Seven Steps of Spiritual Development,* Temple Lodge, London, 2004.

Spirituality and Social Renewal

Books for a New Human Community

As the new millennium begins, no area of activity calls for more visionary thinking than that of social life and community. This is one forgotten element in today's scientific and technological utopia. We can construct great buildings and cities, form multinational corporations, develop sophisticated economic models—but we generally do so at the expense of the human beings, for the sake of whom these things supposedly exist. The result is that our best efforts lead to an increase of human suffering on an ever greater scale.

We recognize that we have moved into a new globalism; that the world is one, economically and geopolitically. Futurists extol the possibilities opened up by the new complex of silicon-based electronic interactive networks, yet, at the same time our ideas about who we are and what we are capable of as human beings remains pitifully inadequate and largely determined by nineteenth-century models. Thus, all talk of "family values," "virtues," and new forms of collaboration and cooperation tends either to miss the point or to reinforce the most regressive aspects of our technology.

This series of books seeks to provide new social insights, perspectives of hope and practical idealism, based on a recognition of the fundamental spiritual nature of human and social life. It explores how we can become more conscious and spiritually responsible creators of community and of a social and economic order that can serve the human future.

Printed in the United States
36115LVS00002B/94-129